Be Here Now

Finding Peace and Joy in the Present Moment

Meredith Gaston Masnata

Hardie Grant
BOOKS

To live is the rarest thing in the world. Most people exist, that is all.
— Oscar Wilde —

We'll have this moment forever, but never ever again.
— Doris Day —

Look past your thoughts, so you may drink the nectar of this moment.
— Rumi —

THIS BOOK
BELONGS TO

....
....
....

Table of Contents

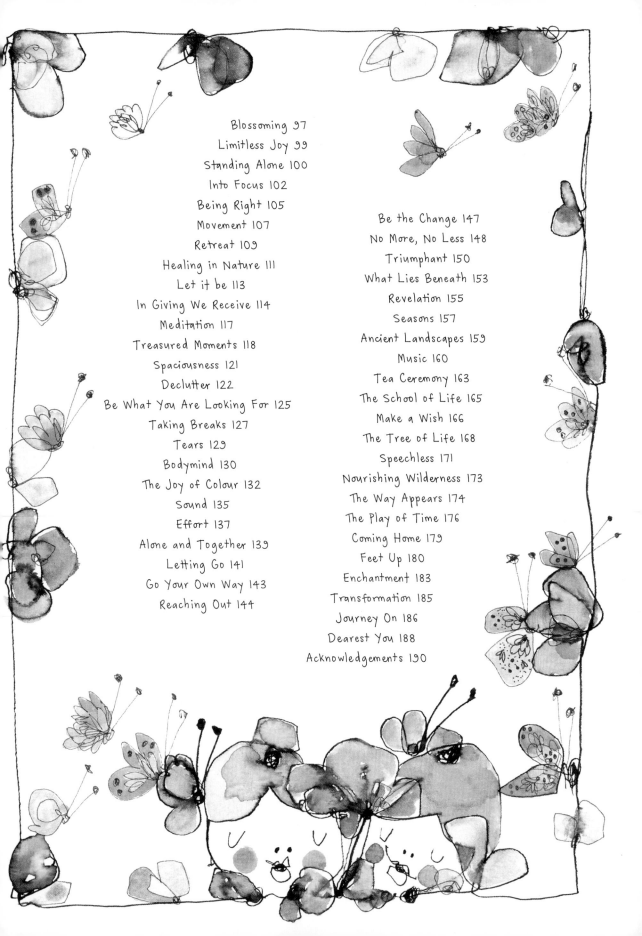

Introduction

Dearest You,

The present moment, still and dynamic all at once, is the only moment we truly have. The past has gone and the future is not assured. Wonderful things worthy of our appreciation happen within and around us in every moment. And yet, all too often we seem to decline our timeless invitation to be here now — to be present. We can find ourselves lost in our thoughts of yesterday or our dreams for tomorrow, wishing to be elsewhere or other than ourselves; becoming consumed by distractions, or simply too busy to savour our lives.

All the while, the beauty, uniqueness and splendour of life await our acknowledgment, our participation, and the attunement of our senses.

Indeed, subtle, nuanced pleasures of all kinds call for our touch and awareness moment to moment, ready to bring greater colour, texture, joy and inspiration to our lives. As we awaken to the richness of life, we ground ourselves into the present moment with gratitude, humility and mindful presence. We enjoy the luscious, luminous gifts of being here now. It soon becomes undeniable that our aliveness is the most precious and wonderful gift we will ever possess, and our mindful presence a present to ourselves and all those with whom we share life.

Some moments are overtly magical and divine, others more quietly and humbly so — from hands warming around tea cups to moments spent savouring the unassuming perfection of a sunset. A heavenly morning, a tender embrace, a deep breath enjoyed in quietude. A raindrop quivering in a spider's web, dappled sunlight kissing leaves, the gentle picking of a flower. Single moments, so lucid and rich, join together to make meaningful lives of beauty, meaning and purpose. With our loving attention, we awaken to the all at once robust, delicate, fleeting and timeless qualities that we human beings share with the world around us. By doing so, we learn the value and joy of life.

The impermanence of the present moment encourages us to see our own impermanence and to live our lives with wonder and appreciation. As we let go of our longing and striving for more — our tendency towards accumulation, diversion, complication and comparison — we free ourselves to experience life in the present moment, as it happens. An entirely new, vivid

and experiential way of life reveals itself to us. We are instantly imbued with freshness — we come alive. We are called to live and let live daily, immersing ourselves fully into life yet letting go of all things, as one present moment lets go into another. Participating in life's miraculous dance, we see that within impermanence exists the comfort and consistency of constant change. Nature shows us so; her moods and shifts, her seasons and her resilience speak to our own. The harmony and tension, stillness and movement that give life to the present moment makes it the most compelling, intoxicating and only moment in which to live.

May the beauty of the present moment and our willingness to participate fully in it change our lives, teach us the profound lessons our spirits are longing to learn, and reveal to us the peace, happiness and wisdom we inherently possess. May the words and pictures within this book encourage you to see the beauty in each moment, and inspire you to make it matter.

in your heart you

Enjoying this book

Here we are, meeting between the covers of this beautiful book and sharing moments in time. This book is composed of a series of moments, lovingly acknowledged and bound together as an ode to the beauty, joy and mystery of life. Your own moments shared in thought and feeling — in celebration of your own creativity, life and dreams — will come into play herein, merging into the shared splendour that is our aliveness. This aliveness is our binding thread: our humanity. And in our gratitude for the inherent magnificence of our being, we become all the more alive. This journal is to be enjoyed just so — as a collaborative celebration.

May these gathered moments encourage you to explore your own creativity and commune with the beauty and inspiration dwelling in your everyday life and world. May you feel moved to notice little things and document them carefully, experiencing your life as a work of art, magical and worthy of your attention. In doing so, you will live in perennial connection with the wonders of your own being, knowing the joy of life on earth.

We are here to live, and the richness of our lives opens up to us when we choose to land willingly in the present moment. May this book gently but unequivocally call you to inhabit the visceral, magical, sensuous and exploratory experience of being human. Within these pages may you see aspects of your own nature and aspirations mirrored back to you as you dive more deeply into all there is to know and love of life.

You might move through these pages from cover to cover or dip in and out at your whim, slowly taking in certain words and pictures over time. You will find numerous, diverse little pieces on subjects from daydreaming to finding spaciousness, cultivating resilience to taking time out and nurturing inner peace. Particular words and pictures may resonate with you on days you might benefit from them, helping you to bring yourself back to this moment — to truly know that you are here, not caught in the past or preoccupied with the future but right here — within the limitless, compelling potential of the timeless now.

10

The present is indeed timeless. As we pause and breathe, we realise that the thinker of our thoughts, the feeler of our feelings, and the busy doer of our deeds is a divine, peaceful and eternal energy beyond time, effortlessly anchored and connected to all there is. In a busy world in which many people are running on automatic, missing their lives, may we be revolutionary in our presence. May we open our eyes and awaken with gratitude and love.

Make a journal of your own. Take photos. Sketch. Write poems. See things. Take a walk on the beach or into the forest. Feel the elements embracing and moving you. Potter through the mountains. Look your pet in the eyes. Hold your lover's hand. Watch the clouds move or study a tree in your garden as it grows. Hear birds sing and bees buzz. Tread gently. Exhale. Take your children into the wild.

Let their imaginations run free as you allow your own to the do the same. We need never grow old in our hearts.

Two self-taught artists created this book in an organic collaboration spanning a year of pottering at home and further afield. But not too far afield. Indeed, all the art and words in this book were generated at home or within just a couple of hours of our sanctuary, demonstrating that great beauty can be found right where we are; it just needs to be seen.

Enjoy this book. Our greatest wish is that it will make you feel alive, inspiring you to create and nurture your very own version of heaven on earth.

Meredith & Roberto

Observation

Choosing to see carefully adds richness to every place and moment. The spaces we inhabit daily can become so familiar to us that we forget to look closely at them — to drink them in with time and care. Colours change before our eyes as light shifts, a breeze ruffles a curtain, natural elements grow and age, and the touch of our hands gives patina to various surfaces. Inanimate objects are more alive than they seem and take on even greater energy and beauty when gifted with our attention. Encouraging our eyes to see afresh each day allows us to be inspired by the world around us, at best enchanted by the way seemingly simple things are: the way they change or stay the same. Observing and enjoying our surroundings allows us to connect more gratefully and meaningfully with them. Over time we become more curious about the spaces we know and love; draw comfort from them, nurture and care for them and, in doing so, find great satisfaction.

14

Imagination

As we move about the world, we may find ourselves glimpsing certain scenes or vignettes that spark our curiosity. Fences behind which secret gardens are growing wild, mysterious little windows to other worlds, open doors we yearn to peek around, scents, sights and sounds unfamiliar to us yet part of others' natural habitats. There is so much our eyes cannot see, especially when we move quickly and busily about without paying attention to our surroundings. All the while, places tell stories. Indeed, there are stories all around us, just waiting for our wits to sharpen and our imaginations to awaken.

With more careful observation, we can live deeply rich and imaginative lives, finding fairytales and fodder for daydreams in all manner of places. Next time you emerge from your familiar surroundings, engage your imagination and creativity by observing details. See cheeky ficus vines making interesting shapes on walls. Watch sunlight dance through stained glass windows. Catch leaf skeletons floating on the breeze, or spot fossilised signatures and love notes in the pavement. As we activate and sharpen our senses, we awaken our imaginations. A new way of being reveals itself as we discover ourselves living in perpetual, moment to moment magic.

Magical Spaces

Should we wish to live magical, enchanting lives of beauty and bliss,
we must create magical, enchanting spaces elevated by beauty and
savoured in blissful appreciation. We must bring our attention to
the sensuality of being and our visceral experience of life in space.
We must bring our attention to light, sound, texture and taste, and
to the touch of things — communing fully with life. In doing so, we
curate a melange of elements, creating stimulating yet harmonious
environments in which we may feel elevated — in which we may find
ourselves not just existing but truly living. The freshness of flowers
gathered around us, the glow of candlelight, the soft touch of drapes,
the shifting light of day through a window — all such sensory delights
speak to the heavenly charm of spaces that awaken and inspire our
spirits. As we deepen our sensitivity and gratitude for life, our inner
worlds, touched by mystery and gorgeousness, are reflected in the
outer spaces we create and inhabit — spaces in living, breathing
expression of our enchantment.

Endless Romance

Endless romance, one of the most beautiful parts of life, is found in choosing a romantic, sensory and sensual way of living. It is to embrace and savour pleasure through beautiful sights, sounds, scents, tastes and textures that elevate our spirits and ignite our senses. Living sensually in endless romance with life changes us. We find ourselves more present and alive, more available to be delighted and consequently more delighted than ever before. The lusciousness and sacredness of life awaits the sharpening and softening of our senses — our attention, appreciation, reverence and praise. And, as we embrace romantic living, we find romance embracing us. Sensual living is a tactile, visceral, inspirational way of being that, with our willingness, becomes an endless romance. And, if we happen to find someone with whom to share our passion in loving communion, we may heighten our joy in unspeakable ways that cause us to know the true essence of heaven on earth. We must first, however, develop a passionate romance between ourselves and life — the first and most important romance we will ever know. So, may we be here now to fall in love — to see, touch, hear, taste and feel the beauty of life. To drink it in, savour it and become it.

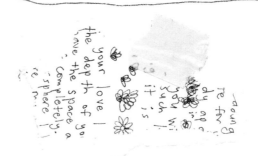

Emergence

Knowing how to move forward in our lives, especially in the face of difficult emotions that cloud our clarity, requires patience and compassion. Mindful living takes time and care. We must honour ourselves and our life stories by making time and taking care through all seasons. In order to emerge from moments or even stretches in darkness into the light — into the brightness of our own light and the greater light of life of which we are all a part — we are called to sit with things. Sit with our feelings tenderly. Sit with our thoughts lovingly. As we call all our thoughts and feelings home, we may embrace them as essential parts of our personal and collective experience of life. Indeed, there is no light without darkness.

No joy without suffering. No coming out without going within. It is the tonality of our lives, the contrasts and textures, the reasons to retreat and the calls to emerge that shape us. In being shaped by life we are gifted and humbled all at once. We are gifted with deeper awareness as we remain open to infinite possibilities for change, growth and bliss, and we are humbled by the depth, breadth and wonder of living. As we sit with ourselves, present and sincere through our difficult times, we find that answers come to us more easily. Our way is illuminated for us; all we must do is be continually willing to turn our faces toward the light, as poet Walt Whitman is thought to have said, letting shadows fall behind us.

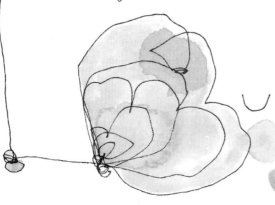

Little Beginnings

From little things big things grow. Yet, too often we are looking for bigger, louder signs and markers of progress to validate and affirm us. In doing so, we overlook many special things: precious, subtle and quite possibly very important little signs of our growth. In what can be a very impatient world, instant gratification can seem very appealing. The bigger the result and the faster we see it, the better. Yet there is no substitute for sincere, concerted and consistent personal effort, nor the intense pleasure and reward garnered through a true journey of learning and discovery. Indeed, the richness of any journey is as satisfying, if not more gratifying, than the destination. Progress savoured little by little over time makes for results with enduring glow and shine. Every little beginning — every little sign of progress made — is to be celebrated. As we journey on, we must take the time to see little things change and blossom, both within and around us. In doing so, we draw meaning, motivation and perennial inspiration from the story of our own life. In the wonderful words of Mother Teresa, 'Be faithful in small things, for it is in them that your strength lies.'

Reverence

In our increasingly busy, modern and secular world, reverence seems rare and precious. It has been said that nothing is sacred any more; that in contemporary humour anything goes; that our all-pervasive visual culture leaves nothing to the imagination; that the wonder and mystery of life has been quantified, measured and made finite by science; and that the value of ancient wisdom has been replaced by a modern tendency to worship information technology, fame and fortune. Many of us find our days lack the depth of culture, the sanctity of rituals and the respectful grace of etiquette to ground, unite and elevate us. We can't quite make sense of our unrest, yet we deeply yearn to feel a sense of belonging and to experience meaning in our lives.

The threads of our humanity come undone when we lose our reverence for the sacredness of life — for wonder, gratitude, tenderness and miracles. By understanding and respecting the profound power of our thoughts, speech and acts, however, we may welcome and grow reverence anew. We can practise reverence in our relationships with ourselves and each other by honouring the preciousness and sanctity of love. We can elevate our language, demonstrate respect, present ourselves thoughtfully, and show appreciation for life in the loving care of our homes, workspaces and natural environments. We can create our own elevating daily rituals: light candles; arrange flowers; sing and dance; even pray. Indeed, we can see that life itself can be lived as prayer — an expression of our appreciation and a celebration of faith in ourselves, life and love. Through decorum, sensitivity, attunement and a true sense of occasion in daily life, we may reinstate reverence, satiating our desire to live meaningful, spiritual lives in a modern world.

Possession

In his beloved book, 'The Little Prince', Antoine de Saint-Exupéry speaks gently to the art of admiring and savouring beautiful things without fixating ourselves upon possessing them. The inclination to possess things can cause us to hold on to more than we truly need to be happy. Our greed blinds us to the abundance we by nature already possess. Indeed, with a little practice, we can observe and treasure the resounding beauty of life at spirit level, then let go into even more beauty, knowing that through appreciative eyes, the magnificence of life is infinite. Moreover, the greatest treasures cannot be touched, even seen, but rather felt in the heart. 'People where you live,' The Little Prince said, 'grow five thousand roses in one garden ... Yet they do not find what they're looking for ... And yet what they're looking for could be found in a single rose ...'

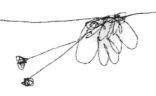

Be Here Now

Let us savour the privilege it is to live upon this earth — seeing,
touching, inhaling, exhaling and exploring each day with love,
appreciation and awareness. May our tenderness, gratitude and care
contribute to the beauty of life and peace on earth. Let us walk in
nature, noticing tiny details, conscious of the infinite miracles unfolding
in our atmosphere. Let us tread gently, humbled and inspired, feeling
nourished and open-hearted to life and, in all these ways, choose to be
here now — truly and completely. We must abandon our indifference,
activate our passion and embrace the magic of living. We must make
time for our earth and learn to prioritise her wellness should we wish to
experience and nurture our own wellbeing. We are created in symbiotic
harmony with nature, but all too often we forget this life-giving
connection and essential truth. Built environments and technology can
distance us from our earth, often causing us to make decisions that
disregard her. Our loving respect for our earth and for life itself
matters more than ever now. May we deepen our love and appreciation
because every moment matters here on earth — there is no time to waste.

Sublimity

The arrestingly divine qualities of true beauty transport us into a higher state of being — a state in which the mysteries of life touch our spirits. The ever-evolving miracles we observe in the natural world around us — the perfection of creation — is our own miraculousness and perfection mirrored back to us. No rose competes with another rose, she is simply the rose. And yet, we human beings tend to compare and contrast, judge and measure, overthink and second guess. The beauty we celebrate in nature, sublime beauty, is a reflection of our own divinity. We too are born of creation and as such, emerge from the very same spring of life. Often blinded to our magnificence, we forget the incredible detail that, like each individual petal of a rose makes it whole, constitutes our own unique design. Touching for a single moment on our sacred aliveness, we come home at last into the bigger picture of life. May such profound awareness of our own being elevate, inspire and encourage us as we choose to dive fully and deeply into life.

At The End of the Day

The sacred beginnings and endings of all our days — dusk and dawn — inspire our awe and call us inward, even if for just a moment. As Buddha teaches, every morning we are born again. What we do today matters most. Similarly, each night we are called to be born into the land of resting, sleeping and dreaming — a universe equally as precious and potent as our waking life. A magical realm in which we are gifted with rich insights, answers and visions of all kinds. The land of our dreams is a world into which we best move in a spirit of peace and harmony at the end of each day. The wonderful naturalist writer Ralph Waldo Emerson is often paraphrased thus: 'Finish each day and be done with it. You have done what you could. Some blunders and absurdities no doubt crept in; forget them as soon as you can. Tomorrow is a new day. You shall begin it serenely and with too high a spirit to be encumbered with your old nonsense.' Before retiring at night, we may express our gratitude for all that we have and all that we are, forgive those who need forgiving, including ourselves, and warmly welcome rest to embrace a new beginning come morning. Approaching each day with such freshness, wonder and grace gifts us lifetimes of fulfilment, joy and inspiration.

No Mud No Lotus

In his exquisite book 'No Mud, No Lotus', Vietnamese Buddhist monk Thich Nhat Hanh describes the way in which the lotus flower — so beautiful, fresh and alive — cannot come into being without the mud from which it springs so gracefully. As such, we are reminded that in emerging from muddy waters — from our doubts and fears, hardships and troubles — we too blossom. Being in the mud of life, while undesirable, teaches us compassion, humility, strength and grace. Just as the darkness of night by contrast makes the stars twinkle, so the darker times we face make the brighter times we savour all the more luminous, precious and sweet. Experiencing our lives as journeys in which each present moment becomes our destination, we are constantly arriving into different seasons. May we learn to welcome the light and shade of our lived experiences in a harmony of our own composition. May we invite the profound lessons and gifts we are unendingly shown each day as we grow, blossoming, bedazzling and triumphing like beautiful lotus flowers.

Into Light

As we move towards greater lightness in our hearts and minds through the peace and joy of mindful living, it becomes easier to notice cloudy thoughts, ideas and beliefs as they cross the sky of our minds. Our power lies in noticing our cloudy thoughts with love, as it is in noticing and interrupting them that we can choose to move in the direction of light instead — to select thoughts that feel more joyous, positive and inspiring for us. Our emotional landscape changes as we are illuminated. While it is essential that we feel our feelings, we will not overcome any unwanted state of being if we fixate upon it, keeping ourselves stuck in its low frequency, the very frequency unsettling, dimming and depleting us. If we wish to be happy, we must consistently choose to move towards light; to embrace a lightness of being; to simplify rather than complicate our thoughts and lives; and to see the lightness and goodness in ourselves, each other and life. We must enjoy humour, levity and play, cultivate positivity, and keep our eyes open to the magic and beauty of life. Habitually brightening our thoughts, we begin to notice that shadows simply cannot lurk in light spaces. No matter what may come our way, there is always light waiting to embrace and illuminate us — indeed enough light to last a lifetime. All we must do is say yes to it.

Being Busy

In our modern world life can be very busy. It is hardly surprising that we can feel overwhelmed yet somehow unable to stop ourselves — as if being busy becomes an expectation, even an addiction. Indeed, some of us wear busyness and exhaustion as badges of honour — signs of a full and successful life. Yet quietude, gentler living and consciously redefining our priorities can offer a whole new picture of richness, success and joy. When we are mindful about our lives and the way we choose to live them, we can consciously create much-needed pockets of peace, stillness and quietude in our days. We can choose to move a little more slowly, insist on quiet time and rest, and be especially conscious of the way we spend the gentler, freer moments we do actually have. Scrolling through news and social media, spending our quiet time as screen time, can make us feel all the more depleted and time poor. Better use of our time inevitably reveals greater expanses of time we have to enjoy; it also helps us to tune into the tone of our own thoughts and feelings, and be with ourselves directly. We soon find that we can lovingly guide our thoughts and feelings in positive and healing directions, bringing greater ease and grace to our hearts, minds and daily lives. As quiet time can be hard to 'find', we must create and relish it with awareness. In our quiet moments, we can focus on all that is good and right within ourselves, our lives and our world. We can close our eyes, meditate, daydream, slow and deepen our breathing, even pray — projecting for our collective peace and joy. While we may feel challenged by the notion, even resist or question the possibility of it, we all truly can slow down if we wish to.

One By One

While many things vie for our attention in any given moment, it is an art to be able to mindfully focus upon that which is right in front of us. When we bring our full selves to each present moment, the future naturally takes care of itself. While we can get so busy building for the future, wealth, success and accolades mean nothing without joyous energy for life in the present moment. Taking things one by one, especially when feeling overwhelmed by multiple commitments or decision fatigue, is essential self-care wisdom. Seeing and experiencing what is right in front of us now means we won't miss the richness of life; that we can make the very most of it and, in doing so, move forward as best as we can, one step at a time. To participate fully in anything we care about — indeed, to truly know what it is that we care about and what matters most to us — we must be right here, right now. With grace and humility, without presumptuousness or pride, we may all live thankfully and mindfully, assessing our prioritising in alignment with our values and making decisions that support our peace and joy as we learn and grow through life. Express your gratitude. Map your dreams. Meditate or sleep on things. Let clarity come as the result of sincere willingness to be happy now. Detangle thought clutter from past and future musings to arrive in this moment. Your wellbeing depends on the vitality of your body, the atmosphere in which you live, and the quality of your relationships with yourself and others. Prioritise and embrace this moment, letting the rest fall into perfect, peaceful place.

 # Quiet Time

Quiet time is delicious, precious time. To enjoy quiet time wisely is to savour relaxing, grounding and nurturing pleasures that invoke a sense of calm within and around us. Such pleasures can become rituals that bring much-needed rejuvenating peace to our days. Quiet time is not about being meaninglessly idle, nor distracting ourselves from our present moment by referring back to a busy world. At best, we make little pockets or longer stretches of conscious, quality quiet time part of each and every day so that we may enjoy the benefits of beautiful, balanced living in touch with ourselves. Indeed, as we quieten down in loving respect for ourselves and life, we can relish feeling truly at home within — the most wonderful feeling we could ever know. We always do and feel better when we are rested and self-connected. It is much easier to find and maintain a calm, clear state of being when we feel peaceful and refreshed.

Through quiet time we replenish our active minds and bodies, restoring ourselves wholly. And, as we learn to rest well, we see that our lives begin to flow with greater ease and grace. When we feel revitalised and at peace, the world around us cannot help but echo our new state. Practising quiet time and experiencing the way it enhances every aspect of our being deepens our sense of gratitude, fulfilment and satisfaction with ourselves and life. In our mindful practice of rest — an inherently encouraging, joyous, inspiring practice — we will find the meaning and motivation we need to answer our daily calls to quietude.

43

Little Signs

The universe speaks to us in a language of its own — a magical, intimate language of signs and symbols. This universal language is as grand and expansive as it is intensely personal. It is a language we all inherently know and understand; it simply requires our attention, recognition and appreciation. Celebrated artist and scholar of life Leonardo da Vinci is often credited with the observation that there are three classes of people: those who see, those who see when they are shown, and those who do not see. In learning how to see, it can be observed that everything connects to everything else. As such, it is hardly surprising that recurring patterns, numbers and visual motifs of all kinds pepper our daily lives, following, mirroring and guiding us, speaking to us in subtle yet powerful and highly intelligent ways. As we become more observant, as we soften and open to life, and as we connect with our intuition through self-care and self-awareness, we efficiently attune our minds to signals from an omniscient universe of which we are part. The more attuned we are to life and living, the more we see, and the more extraordinary, supportive and affirming role little signs begin to play in our daily lives.

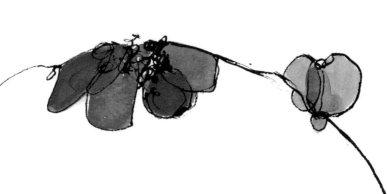

In Time with Life

The beauty of living consciously and mindfully in the present moment — of feeling our feelings and knowing ourselves in grace and truth to honour them — is to realise our emotions at the time of their blossoming: to be at one, and in time, with life. To appreciate the gorgeousness of life, we must be present in it. 'I can only note that the past is beautiful because one never realises an emotion at the time. It expands later, and thus we don't have complete emotions about the present, only about the past,' wrote Virginia Woolf. When we embrace sensations of peace and joy as they feel in their unfolding — not wanting or waiting for more, nor reserving our gratitude for another time, place or space — we allow the immediate emotional experience of each present moment to touch us completely. We needn't wait for the future to appreciate the present in the past. Letting our emotions expand in real time, we may drink in the abundance and richness of life, right now.

Accidentally Zen

As we explore our built and natural environments, we may suddenly stumble across a vision of perfect harmony, quiet symmetry, pure balance and gentle perfection. In Japanese tradition, wabi-sabi is descriptive of organic, often elusive beauty. Wabi-sabi speaks to the inherent perfection in all things, by virtue of the way they naturally are. It celebrates the organic nature of objects, places and spaces with signs of age and use, and understands patina or 'imperfections' as contributions to the essence of beauty. Wabi-sabi recognises subtle feelings emitted by inanimate objects or particular arrangements in space — feelings beyond description, possibly fleeting and timeless all at once. To be aware of the principles of wabi-sabi — which in many ways defies definition but resonates with our spirits — allows us to melt into moments, sights and things that are Zen-like almost by accident, that in their unplanned, natural way, soothe and nourish us.

Delicacy

A delicate word, a soft touch, a gentle, quiet moment alone or together, can be all it takes to gift us the comfort and joy we seek. Oftentimes we anticipate the greatest effect from grandiose gestures or moments, expecting the 'fireworks' of our lives to have the most profound impact upon our spirits. And yet, as celebrated author Jane Austen reminds us, there is no charm equal to tenderness of heart. The delicate, subtle intimate moments we live and share, born of tender thoughts and loving intentions — humble, quiet, kind and beautiful moments — may become our most precious, unforgettable and life-changing experiences of love. May we learn to grow and blossom through the softer, subtler moments in our lives, acquainting ourselves with a delicate new kind of bliss.

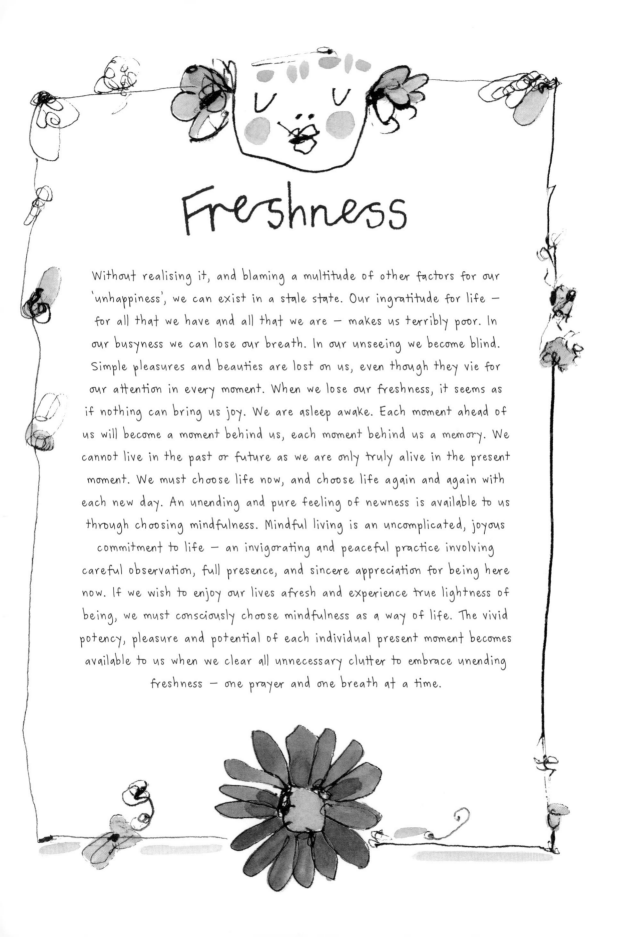

Freshness

Without realising it, and blaming a multitude of other factors for our 'unhappiness', we can exist in a stale state. Our ingratitude for life — for all that we have and all that we are — makes us terribly poor. In our busyness we can lose our breath. In our unseeing we become blind. Simple pleasures and beauties are lost on us, even though they vie for our attention in every moment. When we lose our freshness, it seems as if nothing can bring us joy. We are asleep awake. Each moment ahead of us will become a moment behind us, each moment behind us a memory. We cannot live in the past or future as we are only truly alive in the present moment. We must choose life now, and choose life again and again with each new day. An unending and pure feeling of newness is available to us through choosing mindfulness. Mindful living is an uncomplicated, joyous commitment to life — an invigorating and peaceful practice involving careful observation, full presence, and sincere appreciation for being here now. If we wish to enjoy our lives afresh and experience true lightness of being, we must consciously choose mindfulness as a way of life. The vivid potency, pleasure and potential of each individual present moment becomes available to us when we clear all unnecessary clutter to embrace unending freshness — one prayer and one breath at a time.

Changing Tides

Active self-care in daily life equips us to know ourselves truly and intimately, and to interpret our unique needs and desires in any moment. Appreciating and nourishing our minds, bodies and spirits as we grow and change is a divine privilege granted to us by virtue of our aliveness. As tides inevitably and necessarily change in our lives, we are called to pivot, expand our vision, and dive more deeply into learning as we ride the waves. We can all learn to treasure ourselves with unconditional kindness and compassion. Savouring quiet time alone or cosy, early nights, reading, writing, drawing, meditating, snuggling with pets, taking rest and relaxing, are acts of self-care as much as stretching, mindful walking, singing and dancing. Self-care needn't be expensive or fussy. Rather, and as with most things, simple is best. Building a diverse repertoire of self-care resources that work especially well for us, tailor-made to our natures and needs, ensures that we will be able to fortify, comfort and nurture ourselves every day, even, and especially, during challenging times, big changes or unexpected journeys. Indeed, we needn't ever feel all at sea when we realise that our own love — the most powerful of all loves — is always ready to hold and carry us.

Seeing Beauty

When we observe life with care, we can find magic and beauty in the most unexpected of places. As we elevate our way of seeing, our preconceived notions of beauty naturally shift and expand. Gifting our mindful attention to details, our eyes learn to appreciate all manner of gorgeousness around us. Even the natural charm of seemingly simple things becomes all the more enchanting as our curiosity grows and our senses awaken. Through attentive seeing, unsung objects, places and spaces can take on a life and sparkle of their own. Like detectives, with eyes trained to pick up the finest of details, we sharpen our wits to narratives and signs of life beyond an immediate frame. Who might have sat here last and when? What is growing in and out of these little pots? What spider has spun a web here, snail left a trail there? ... What leaves, blossoms and little seeds have blown in from nearby flora to bring new life to this place? ... Has rain just fallen? ... By cultivating mindful attention in the present moment, our lives organically become more meaningful and enriching to live. By seeing more carefully, we invite all kinds of beauty in life to delight us.

Yesterday Today Tomorrow

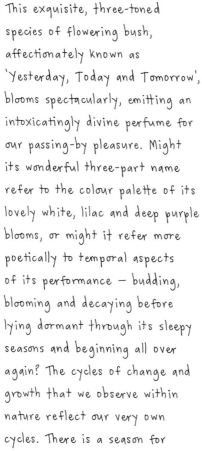

This exquisite, three-toned species of flowering bush, affectionately known as 'Yesterday, Today and Tomorrow', blooms spectacularly, emitting an intoxicatingly divine perfume for our passing-by pleasure. Might its wonderful three-part name refer to the colour palette of its lovely white, lilac and deep purple blooms, or might it refer more poetically to temporal aspects of its performance — budding, blooming and decaying before lying dormant through its sleepy seasons and beginning all over again? The cycles of change and growth that we observe within nature reflect our very own cycles. There is a season for everything: a time for us to grow, a time for us to blossom and perform, a time for us to shed what we no longer need to hold onto and, thereafter, take time to rest and restore before blossoming again. As we move through life, our todays will tomorrow be yesterdays, our tomorrows one day todays. Choosing to be here right now, and living with an awareness of true beauty, which by nature is timeless, we are imbued not only with endless inspiration but with greater peace and perspective in the face of constant change. Invoking the naturalist Ralph Waldo Emerson, we may adopt the rhythm of nature, whose secret is patience.

Right Place, Right Time.

Life has a great deal to do with timing, and good timing — as
random and magical as it may seem — has a great deal to do with
us. When we are open to life and to possibilities — when we choose
love, wonder, humility and integrity, when we embrace kindness,
peace and joy — we always find ourselves in the right place at the
right time. We always land on our feet. Experiencing the delight
of perfect timing, we find all the more reason to deepen our faith
in life's very own way. We find ourselves in fortuitous situations,
meaningful conversations and powerful moments in which all our
stars align, and in which the world hums along with us.
Co-creativity with the energy of life is the key to perfect timing.
We must be awake, willing and ready for life if we wish to
commune with its endless magic. We must improve our relationship
with time itself, heightening our gratitude for time and using it
wisely. We must pursue our inspirations, explore our passions and
live our dreams. And, when we find ourselves touched by joyous
serendipity, we must give thanks. In our gratitude we reinforce our
alignment with, and faith in, life. Goodness, lightness and ever-
perfect timing become ours to enjoy when we choose to live in true
grace, sincere effort and joyful trust.

Heaven on Earth

In our busy world — a world in which we are privy to dense and difficult news, injustices of all kinds, our own and others' hardships — our belief in the possibility of heaven on earth can be greatly challenged. Irrespective of our circumstances, heaven on earth begins with us. Just as the words of a certain boat-rowing lullaby remind us, '... life is but a dream'; we create our realities with our thoughts and as such, our lives become as magical and meaningful as we choose to see and make them. To cultivate heaven on earth, we must choose love for ourselves, each other and nature.

We must comfort and inspire ourselves with positive, healing thoughts and ideas, actively choosing to strengthen our faith in life and love each step of the way. To lose hope in goodness, rightness and beauty is to lose our inner sparkle. Our sparkle, however, can always be rekindled and, in its rekindling, imbue us with even greater strength, faith, peace and joy. In his celebrated work, 'Walden', naturalist Henry David Thoreau writes, 'Heaven is under our feet as well as over our heads.' May we live on our earth as if already in heaven, embracing the tremendous magic of life.

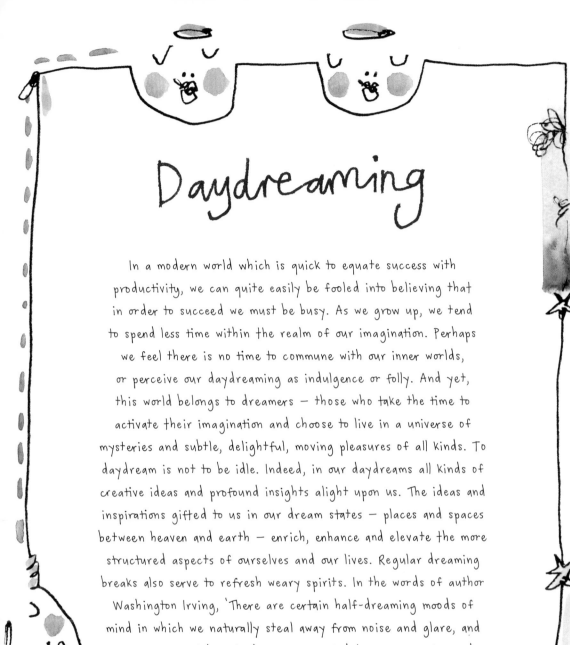

Daydreaming

In a modern world which is quick to equate success with productivity, we can quite easily be fooled into believing that in order to succeed we must be busy. As we grow up, we tend to spend less time within the realm of our imagination. Perhaps we feel there is no time to commune with our inner worlds, or perceive our daydreaming as indulgence or folly. And yet, this world belongs to dreamers — those who take the time to activate their imagination and choose to live in a universe of mysteries and subtle, delightful, moving pleasures of all kinds. To daydream is not to be idle. Indeed, in our daydreams all kinds of creative ideas and profound insights alight upon us. The ideas and inspirations gifted to us in our dream states — places and spaces between heaven and earth — enrich, enhance and elevate the more structured aspects of ourselves and our lives. Regular dreaming breaks also serve to refresh weary spirits. In the words of author Washington Irving, 'There are certain half-dreaming moods of mind in which we naturally steal away from noise and glare, and seek some quiet haunt where we may indulge our reveries and build our air castles undisturbed.' One might then be urged to remember Henry David Thoreau's poignant assertion, 'If you have built castles in the air, your work need not be lost; that is where they should be. Now put the foundations under them.'

Magical Light

To truly appreciate the magic, beauty and embrace of light is to receive a moment-to-moment gift of inspiration part and parcel with our aliveness. As we sharpen our senses, heighten our observation and deepen our gratitude for life on earth, we come to see that light — something we often take for granted — possesses unending powers of enchantment. Indeed, light elevates our senses and touches every aspect of our vitality. Wake at dawn to watch the sun illuminate the first flowers, the tips of leaves and the tips of your fingers. Observe the sun high in the sky to see the world come alive in full colour and, as it moves, pay attention to the shadows, shapes, sunny pockets and cosy corners it creates. Notice the way light moves across water, revealing diamonds upon the ocean and reeds swaying sweetly together in riverbeds. Watch light potter through the canopy of a forest, dance through windows and across walls, move through objects of all kinds and caress your skin with its glow. Come nightfall, observe the light show of sunset. Savour the subtlety of evening light and watch the world as it starts to quieten down. Notice yourself quietening down. Light a candle. Illuminate your space and awaken your senses. Be with light. Notice light. Step into the light and give thanks for light. You will find yourself perpetually nourished in deep connection with the rhythm, mystery and beauty of daily life here on earth.

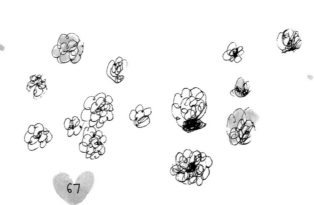

Humanity

Love in the humblest of gestures is the most moving love there is. No fancy gift could touch the heart like a sincere love letter. No elaborate, costly bouquet could possess quite the same charm as a hand-picked posy; a holding hand; a cup of tea; a gentle word. These are the things that matter most: nourishing things that speak to our hearts. It is fascinating that the poorest people on earth tend to be the most unthinkingly generous. In places in which families can hardly afford food, strangers can be welcomed, treated as honoured guests and served tea. In such tenderness — such sincere pride and richness of spirit — we are touched by humanity. In sensing our shared humanity, we find ourselves home at last.

69

Beauty

True beauty stimulates us at a spiritual level, uplifting and enchanting us with inspiration. Endeavouring to see and create a beautiful world around us is a life-affirming, mindful and respectful way of life. To aspire to dwell within a beautiful environment and to connect meaningfully with our own beauty, the beauty of others and the majesty of our natural world is unto itself a reason for being. In our pursuit and cultivation of beauty, we express our gratitude for the unending magic of life. It is a privilege afforded to us as human beings to experience beauty sensorily: to be sentient beings in a living, breathing, feeling universe brimming with visual treasures and infinite, subtle delights. Subjective by nature, our experience of beauty is intensely personal.

What enchants our eyes may be unappealing to others, and what others see and understand as beautiful may surprise or even baffle us. And herein lies the tremendous intimacy of beauty as a spiritual communion with the energy of life and the energy of inspiration: while beauty is as nuanced and varied as we are, our perception of it and feeling is universal. Bringing beauty into our worlds can be done with great care and time, such as the commissioning of a resplendent bouquet, each bloom carefully considered, or it can be as simple as picking a single flower to admire and savour with appreciation. Indeed, beauty is for everyone. It needn't be complicated, costly or inaccessible. Notice a tiny flower springing up from a footpath as you walk by, and you will see beauty's willingness to permeate any and every space — motivating, stimulating and awakening our hearts.

70

Inner Peace

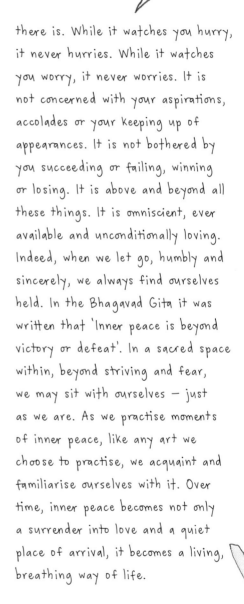

Inner peace is the greatest gift we could ever possess. It is a gift we can find and feel only now — in the present moment. Inner peace cannot be relegated to the past — a time no longer ours to live. Nor can it be suspended in space for an uncertain future in which things feel perfectly settled — in which all our needs are met. If we cannot allow ourselves the gift of inner peace in the present moment, it will always elude us. As such, inner peace is a moment-to-moment matter of choice. Close your eyes and breathe now. Let your hurries and worries melt into every inhale and exhale. Beneath the whirring of agendas and busy to-do lists rests a consciousness aware of all our thoughts and feelings. This consciousness is always peaceful. It is connected to all life, and connects us with everyone and everything

there is. While it watches you hurry, it never hurries. While it watches you worry, it never worries. It is not concerned with your aspirations, accolades or your keeping up of appearances. It is not bothered by you succeeding or failing, winning or losing. It is above and beyond all these things. It is omniscient, ever available and unconditionally loving. Indeed, when we let go, humbly and sincerely, we always find ourselves held. In the Bhagavad Gita it was written that 'Inner peace is beyond victory or defeat'. In a sacred space within, beyond striving and fear, we may sit with ourselves — just as we are. As we practise moments of inner peace, like any art we choose to practise, we acquaint and familiarise ourselves with it. Over time, inner peace becomes not only a surrender into love and a quiet place of arrival, it becomes a living, breathing way of life.

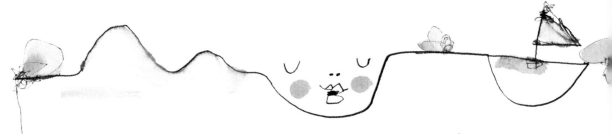

Into The Wild

Doing things the same way every day is like opening a book and reading only one page. As we mix things up — explore, try new things, welcome adventures, open our hearts and minds to learning and discovery — we find ourselves refreshed. New inspirations become ours to savour and translate with creativity, and we are reminded to open our eyes to life: to all the compelling details of the present moment. We needn't go into the wild to break our routine. Simply taking a different route to a familiar destination, visiting a place we haven't been before, listening to new music, choosing new words or trying a new recipe are ways to reinvigorate our senses and welcome freshness into our lives. Beyond all that is familiar — beyond our comfort zone — wait infinite experiences to grow and delight us. We can all too easily become stuck in routines and perform large parts of our days as if on automatic pilot. Living this way, it is hardly surprising that we feel the present moment unworthy of our full attention: we have done it all before, there is nothing new to see. And yet, as we choose to enter the wilderness of the unknown as often as possible, we condition our eyes to see again. And as we condition our eyes to see again, we inspire our hearts and minds anew. Helen Keller wrote that the only thing worse than being blind is to have vision but not see. In awakening to life, we must sharpen our wits with variety, deviate from our theme, and grow true willingness to explore.

Resilience

Cultivating resilience allows us to move through our days with a grounding sense of strength and comfort from within, and to tread with equal measures of strength and softness through our relationships and our world. No matter what may come, by cultivating resilience we find reservoirs of perseverance, positivity and courage ever available to us. If we perceive resilience as hardness or impenetrability, however, we miss its essence and beauty. While resilience gives us strength, it flourishes with our willingness to be tender, flexible and open. This concept is beautifully expressed in the nature of the thistle. Just as the thistle flower's prickly pod is self-protective, we must actively preserve our peace in daily life by carefully choosing the thoughts we think, the words we speak and the actions we take. We must be selective with the company we choose to keep, nurture loving inner atmospheres, and work with personal boundaries that nurture and support us. Yet we needn't harden ourselves to life and each other, feeling as if we always have to be strong even when we need to surrender, know the answers when we simply don't, or turn down loving assistance when we sincerely need it. Our prickly buds must break before we can blossom too. Indeed, to truly blossom, we must see and experience ourselves with respect and compassion as we grow and change. And this courageous openness is resilience.

Celebrating Others

Delighting in the accomplishments, successes and happiness of others is an important part of life and essential for our own experience of joy. When we watch others soar and we celebrate them, we soar too. When we watch others succeed begrudgingly, we keep ourselves small. We all came here with different natures and different gifts to share, and our life stories are a series of choices we make. When we make choices in alignment with our hearts and our innermost values, we fly. Looking more deeply into the luminous success of others we invariably find stories of hard work, integrity and sincere endeavour. Stories of falling down seven times and getting up eight (as the Chinese proverb goes) hold visions of positive outcomes even in the face of adversity and disappointment, and, perhaps most importantly, an unwavering sense of faith in oneself. Indeed, flying takes faith and courage. As the poet Alfred Lord Tennyson reminds us, the shell must break before the bird can fly. Rather than enviously looking upon others in full, wondrous flight, may we be the first to cheer, the first to celebrate, and the first to feel inspired by the infinite possibilities life gifts us to soar.

At Home Within

At home within we find the peace we seek. While we may expend great amounts of time and energy searching near and far beyond us for the joy of love and the bliss of belonging, when we come home to ourselves, we come home at last. As we begin to spend time nurturing our inner worlds in gentle ways, we may well realise that we have spent a long time running away from home: from a person we thought we might not like — a person we may have forgotten to love, even forgotten how to love. We too often neglect to fully acquaint ourselves with who we truly are, forget to show ourselves compassion, and savour very little quiet time alone. Busying ourselves with life and other people's business, we displace precious energy from self-awareness and self-connection. Diverting our attention, projecting our thoughts and feelings without embodying and integrating them, even living vicariously through others, we take circuitous routes on our forever paths home. Yet we can ease our way very simply by being with ourselves lovingly — showing ourselves the tenderness, respect and compassion we would show our most loved ones — letting ourselves feel loved by ourselves. As we soften into our own love we find our hurts healing, our old defences melting, and our true selves here right now to love and care for us, at home at last.

Inner Summer

'In the depth of winter,' wrote celebrated writer and philosopher Albert Camus, 'I finally learned that within me there lay an invincible summer.' In our wintery, dark moments, it can be easy to forget that glowing within us is a brilliant, inextinguishable light beyond space and time. This light is the luminous and timeless spirit of life: our eternal life force and truest essence. Sufi mystic Rumi teaches that the entire universe is inside us. What we seek is seeking us, most especially love and joy. As figments of the great spirit of life, each and every human being contains the past, present and future: all seasons and weather conditions, all mystery, beauty and truth. Indeed, the light, inspiration and happiness that we seek lies potently and magically within us like an endless summer. And yet, within ourselves can be the very last place that we look for love and joy, especially when our faith and feelings are ruffled. Gently sensing our invincible summer within each day, we may move through all life's seasons with greater resilience, faith, perspective and grace.

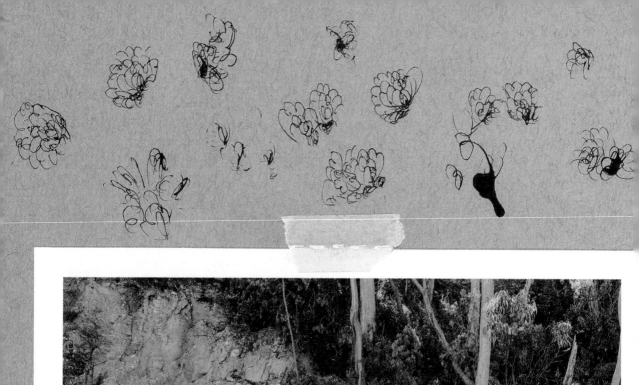

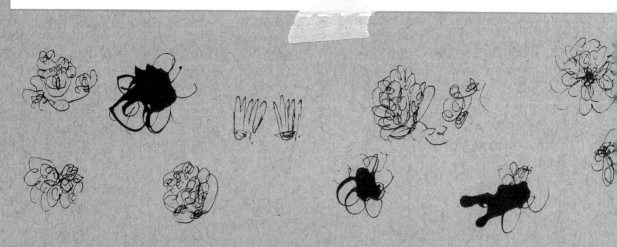

Nature Therapy

It is a joy to realise that we can come home to ourselves and, indeed,
heaven, every time we reconnect with nature. Nature's therapies
nourish our joy and awaken our senses, offering dazzling benefits
that we may not even realise are readily available to us. In nature
we find comfort, solace, inspiration and healing. Nature's therapies
include activities such as earthing: placing our bare feet upon the
earth and absorbing its energising natural ions to ground us and
support our wellbeing; forest bathing: immersing ourselves in the
luscious green life and healing depth of the forest; ocean bathing:
cleansing and rejuvenating in salt water; mindful walking and even
mindful sunbathing, all of which serve to awaken and enliven our
bodies. In its wordless, profound way, nature speaks to us, offering us
the peace and comfort we can find ourselves seeking but not finding
in so many other ways — through acquiring things, distracting
ourselves, or abandoning our present moment. In nature we are called
to be here now — breathe in all that surrounds us, notice details
and immerse ourselves in the sensory experience that is our aliveness.
Indeed, as living, breathing human beings we are not separate
to nature: we are part of nature. To harmonise with nature is to
harmonise with ourselves and to reap the healing, fortifying and
nurturing benefits of coming home.

Enjoy the View

We must cultivate enthusiasm for life and the world. We must be observant and intermingle with the world around us in ways that satiate our curiosity, grow our inspiration and inspire our wonder. Boredom is an unthinkable and impossible state for an open, willing and grateful mind. We naturally impoverish our spirits when we close our eyes to life, busying ourselves with infinite distractions that pull us from the present moment. In its sublime, ever-changing and ever-giving way, the immediate world around us is always enough. The deficit is in our gratitude, sensitivity and keen observation, not in any shortcoming on our world's part. Taking joyous responsibility for the way we bring the world into view, our world comes alive and so do we. W.B. Yeats is credited with these sentiments: 'The world is full of magic things, patiently waiting for our senses to grow sharper.' Enjoy your view.

Home

Grateful, mindful living makes life a joy. Nowhere more so than at home — our most intimate, daily place. Cocooned from the outside world, home becomes an anchoring microcosm in which to dream, rest, create and play. We house our treasures, enjoy familiar routines, nurture ourselves, and care for the people and things we love. As we learn to see and appreciate the little pleasures of home life as great gifts, we begin to derive pleasure from the simplest of things. And to derive pleasure from the littlest, most uncomplicated and commonplace of things is the secret to sustainable happiness. 'The power of finding beauty in the humblest things' wrote Louisa May Alcott, 'makes home happy and life lovely.'
Snuggling into a sofa, setting a table, making a bed, patting a pet, hanging an artwork, tucking in the chairs, fluffing the pillows, watering the plants — any and all such homely activities may be elevated and celebrated with our loving attention to detail. Living in grateful reverence for our home life, we find ourselves feeling comforted and enriched. Indeed, to practise and savour mindfulness at home, to imbue our home with thoughtfulness and care, is to actively create an inhabitable expression of our love — to live in a little heaven of our very own.

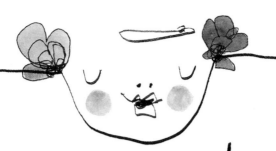

Document

Making art is not reserved for artists. Words are not reserved for writers. We needn't be dancers to dance, musicians to make music, or chefs to create in the kitchen. Indeed, from crafting objects of beauty and curiosity to making music, writing love notes or thank you letters, writing the stories of our lives or crafting fairytales from thin air, we are creative beings born of creative energy in an infinitely creative universe calling for our daily participation. Inspiration surrounds us in every moment. Oftentimes we deny our creativity because we are stifled by perfectionism and self-limiting beliefs. We fixate upon outcomes, seeing creativity as a means to an end. All the while, the true pleasure, magic and joy of creativity is in the creative process. The process — the doing and making of things — is the making of us. We are all invited to grow through exercising and exploring the unending creativity that is our birthright, not relegating it to a world beyond our own but integrating it into our daily lives and personalities. Document your life. Journal; craft; try drawing and painting, reserving all judgement. Write a song or a story, just because. Free yourself to explore your inner world, expressing yourself by using your hands in tune with your heart and mind. Bring your life to life. Your very own unique expression is one of a kind. May you treasure this truth, and come to experience your innate creativity in a whole new way, starting right now.

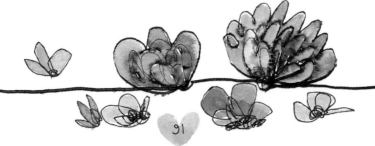

The Break of Day

Witnessing the break of day, we come alive in quite a special way — a way that connects us to nature, our own rhythms and the rhythms of our natural world. Our modern, built environments, with artificial light, gadgets to exacerbate our restlessness and the demands of work and home, culminate in many of us waking — startled — to our alarm clocks, ready or unready to 'do it all over again'. We can feel disenchanted by — even begrudging of — a new day. Like other ancient traditions offering timeless wisdom for modern living, the science of life, Ayurveda, suggests that attuning ourselves to nature's rhythms helps us to balance our own biorhythms, supporting our vitality, peace and joy. Many of us rise and check the news or social media, immediately detuning from the present moment, from our own thoughts and feelings, and from our earth and aliveness. We set a tone for our day that speaks of distraction and absence rather than gratitude and presence. To savour the majestic, wondrous experience of dawn, a daily gift, we must choose to be present; to witness the first light shift in a kaleidoscope of soft and vivid colours; to watch the stars and moon melt into a new sky; to hear the first sounds of the day — birds singing, people moving, wind blowing, rain falling, sheets rustling — and then to feel our bodies in time and space; to feel ourselves as part of the tenderness, sacredness and gentleness of each new day, before the hustle and bustle of it all begins. As best as we possibly can, quietening down at dusk and rising to dawn allows us to live in conscious harmony with nature and, in turn, with ourselves.

Being Seen

For some, being seen is a great pleasure. When the limelight calls, participation is a joy. For others however, being seen prompts feelings of great vulnerability. To be looked at feels exposing: to be seen and judged. And yet, living our lives authentically, guided by unwavering values of sincerity and self-respect, we understand that the way others choose to see us is by no means defining of us. When we are true to ourselves and hold our own, we realise that the person we see in our own eyes, our own self — the way we see and experience ourselves — is what matters most. Everything else is literally extraneous.

Indeed, others' thoughts say more about them than they do about us. When we realise that what other people think of us is simply their business, not ours, we are liberated and empowered for life. The weight of others' scrutiny and judgement diminishes into something of very little consequence to us, like proverbial water off a duck's back. After all, when we love what we do and simply get on with things, we needn't be waiting for others' approval or disapproval. In a busy, over-exposed and often brash world, humility, perseverance, self-respect and respect for one's own privacy are qualities to be valued. While some of us may never love to be seen, we can love ourselves enough to transform our experience of it and flourish our own way.

Blossoming

Poet Anaïs Nin noticed that there comes a time at which the risk we take in blossoming is less than the risk taken by staying tightly held back in our buds — that our lives expand and contract according to our courage. Indeed, we all reach very powerful points in life in which we are ripe for transformational growth. At such times, we are being called to break through inertia and face our resistance to blossoming. This can naturally cause us quite a mix of feelings, some rather unexpected. We might notice the euphoria of positive change and an inner knowingness of our profound personal growth. We might notice ourselves feeling a little worried or fearful of the unknown, as we face departing from a familiar and quite possibly comfortable old version of reality we have just outgrown. We may also observe an odd, tugging sense of sadness and loss as, while blossoming is what we are born to do, we can grieve old versions of ourselves and the limiting old habit patterns and beliefs that used to keep us small and quite possibly, to our old minds, keep us safe. Yet, in blossoming, we see that life always rises up to meet and support us as we grow. May we observe that flowers blossom not in fear or comparison with any other flower, nor with self-consciousness or vanity. Flowers bloom because growing and flourishing is naturally part of their design, just as it is part of ours. Let us celebrate the fullness of our potential as we grow and change.

Limitless Joy

Joy is a limitless energy. We often stand in the way of joy with redundant, illusory thoughts of being unworthy and undeserving of it, or with a limited understanding of joy as inherently fleeting, even unrealistic. Yet we were not born to suffer. As Rumi reminds us, we were born with wings. Why would we wish to crawl through life? 'Could I be happy? Could my happiness last?' Yes. By nurturing gratitude and presence in our daily lives we actively create conditions for joy to flourish — joy that is deeply nourishing and truly enduring. The life-affirming experience of joy — an exquisite experience that fills our minds, bodies and spirits with comfort, vitality and peace — is available to us all. Joy is not selective; rather, it is born of a thoughtful inner climate. As we love and care for ourselves, we embody joy. As we grow and celebrate our joy, we find that we have joy to share, like flowers we may gift to those around us, simply by virtue of our presence. While old, self-imposed limitations may befuddle us, in clarity we see and know that joy is limitless — right here and now. Joy in the present; joy as we grow and change; and joy as our dreams come true.

Standing Alone

It is absolutely necessary that we learn to stand alone in strength and grace when life calls us to do so. When we take the time to know, respect and align with our true values and beliefs, it is necessary that we stand by them and stand by ourselves, even when challenged. While at times we may be ridiculed or doubted for our thoughts and feelings, the courage to be ourselves — to believe in ourselves and be true to ourselves — is character defining and an aspirational choice that we all have the power to make. When we honour ourselves by embracing our individuality and uniqueness, we feel liberated to express ourselves authentically, even if that means stepping away from the crowd and standing alone. In standing alone and standing tall, we naturally rise above criticism and negativity and, from a higher place, endeavour to keep seeing ourselves and life as crisply and clearly as possible. Writer Ralph Waldo Emerson observed that, 'To be yourself in a world that is constantly trying to change you is the greatest accomplishment.' May your ultimate gift be living your own true life.

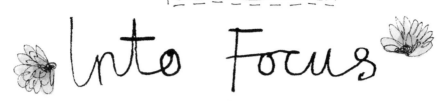

Into Focus

When facing a task at hand, especially one over which we might have been procrastinating, we are wise to bring our attention into very sharp focus. A short time given to a task with our full, focused attention is much more effective and rewarding than a long time labouring over the same task with our scattered attention, begrudging attitude and mental absence. Clear the slate of your mind by taking a few deep breaths and visualise the task in front of you with a sense of clarity and calm. Consider what needs to be done and the way you will go about doing it. Next, visualise the task completed to a very high standard. Sense the satisfaction you will feel, and allow this satisfaction to motivate you as you make a start. Should you be facing something like paperwork, set the scene. Clean your space, put on some beautiful classical music, make a pot of tea, even light a candle. Make your task as pleasant and joyous as possible with a carefully planned atmosphere and focused mindset. Soon you will find that accomplishing any task, from paying bills to washing the dishes, can become an opportunity to sharpen your wits, feel good and truly enjoy your life.

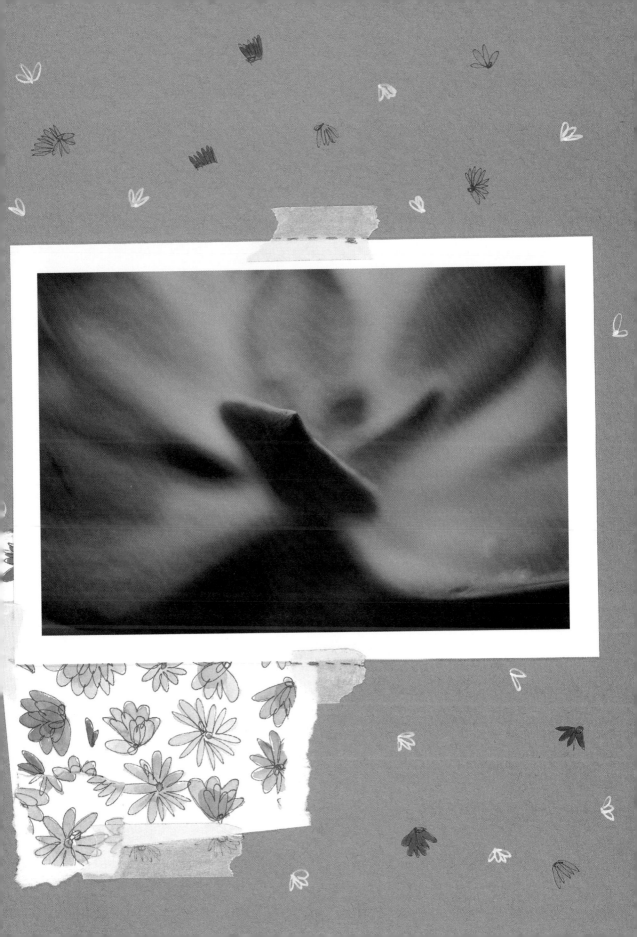

Being Right

We can become so preoccupied with being right that we forget to be happy. Indeed, we can put our need to be right before happiness and harmony, making our lives, and the lives of those with whom we share our time, unnecessarily difficult. Whether we see it or not, we often get stuck in conversations of blame, shame, guilt and righteousness — dialogues both spoken and internal. Yet there is always peace, lightness and grace in relinquishing our need to be right — to win an argument, for instance, or to somehow know better than others, thereby making ourselves bigger and them smaller. While we may find temporary satisfaction in being 'right' or 'winning', when we look more closely, we see that no argument is a winning matter. The person fixated upon being right is losing time, energy and perspective, even others' respect. The person being wronged is losing joy, quite possibly even balance and confidence. Happiness is not found in being righteous or 'right'. It is found in being open-minded and open-hearted: ready to listen and ready to learn. When we embrace life in the present moment, we understand the continual need to let go of all things, liberating ourselves and others to enjoy the very best of life without losing precious time on relative minutiae that impoverish our spirits and steal our joy. Let us choose love instead. In the words of Sufi mystic Rumi: 'Out beyond ideas of wrongdoing and rightdoing there is a field. I'll meet you there. When the soul lies down in that grass, the world is too full to talk about.'

Movement

A crucial part of illuminating, fulfilling and energising ourselves in daily life is attention to movement — an active appreciation for the experience of our bodies in space. Loving and caring for our bodies is our lifelong privilege. The artist Egon Schiele observed, 'Bodies have their own light which they consume to live: they burn, they are not lit from the outside.' To be sure, as movement generates energy, moving our bodies generates more energy for us to enjoy. We may translate this vital energy into loving ourselves and one another, into creative endeavours of all kinds: deep learning, meaningful contribution to life, and the cultivation of resounding wellness that glows from within us. Honouring our physical bodies each day means tending to them and caring for them with mindful eating, joyous movement, careful grooming, ample rest and deep relaxation. Our wonderful bodies, capable of so many things, love be exercised, explored and enjoyed to the fullest. As we move our bodies, we actively shift old energy while generating fresh, new energy. We become the beneficiaries of the inherent biochemical processes stimulated within us to naturally enhance our joy and vitality. While moving may some days take effort, even discipline, it always gifts us with revitalising rewards. The stronger and more flexible we are in our bodies, the stronger and more flexible we may be in our minds. Indeed, the mind and body move and work together in splendid, perpetual synergy — and in what is the greatest dance of our lives.

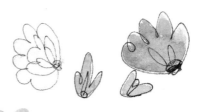

Retreat

Retreating is essential for each one of us in our busy world. Taking time away from our day-to-day lives and realities, whether it be for just a few hours, days or even weeks, and retreating into nature, at best with very limited connection to the outside world, offers us a true reprieve. We must regularly retreat to reconnect with ourselves, reclaim control of our state of being and reclaim our serenity. We inherently know that disconnecting is part of reconnecting and that taking time to quieten the noise of busy places, busy agendas and busy minds is balm for our spirits. As such, let us feel encouraged to seek out and frequent quiet, peaceful places in which we can simply be with ourselves. We may initially find that we have brought a lot of noise with us, and settling down might feel impossible. Alas, we must simply continue to be with ourselves. We must exercise loving self-discipline, firmly resisting the urge to plug back in to a constant stream of distractions distancing us from ourselves, nature and life in the present moment. We soon notice that the constant stream of distractions that can all too often eclipse our realities is as all-pervasive as we make it and allow it to be. Quietude is rich, therapeutic and profound. Within simplicity and peace, the beauty of what matters most in life expands, crowding out the clutter of less consequential things. We find our perspective balancing and our priorities shifting in favour of our truest wellness — our inner peace.

Healing in Nature

Deep healing begins in nature — our natural habitat and our home. Returning to nature we find strength and solace — a timeless sense of belonging, and an awareness of the endless miracles amongst which we live. Since the dawn of time, human beings have drawn upon natural remedies for healing purposes, including plant medicines, stones and crystals, the energy of the sun, moon and stars, even the potent essence of sacred sites. Not relegated solely to the world of alternative medicines, we may be surprised to learn that the majority of allopathic, pharmaceutical medicines are derived from plants, too, from aspirin (willow tree bark) to morphine (the poppy) to caffeine (found in coffee beans, cacao pods and tea leaves), which is used to treat migraines and fatigue. Ancient Egyptians would take aromatherapeutic baths with herbs, flowers and crystals; ancient Greeks enjoyed massage with plant extracts distilled into oils. Apothecaries of ancient times brimmed with potent plant medicines in bottled herbal tonics, the recipes for which modern naturopaths still draw upon today.

Native cultures, including Aboriginal and Torres Strait Islander Peoples, have cultivated profoundly respectful and intimate relationships with our earth, not only knowing country in a geographical sense but very much aware of the unique properties of various earthly offerings such as flowers, fruits, nuts and seeds for healing the mind and body; remedies to soothe upset stomachs or for contraceptive measures; elixirs for healing wounds or settling headaches. Even the herbs we use daily in cooking, from basil and thyme to rosemary and oregano, possess inherent healing properties to boost our wellbeing and enliven our senses. We are quite commonly aware of drawing on lavender for relaxation, aloe vera to soothe the skin and digestive system, and chamomile to calm the mind. More than just an exquisite flower we may pass by, echinacea, growing here in wild abundance, is treasured for its ability to reduce the severity of colds and flu and to support our immune systems. May we take the time to cultivate greater wisdom within our natural world, growing our respect for our earth and stepping into a whole new realm of wellbeing.

Let it be

Perfection is an organic expression. Live and let live with grace. Be yourself freely and allow others the same peace and joy. Observe the gorgeous wildness in nature — an unbridled, imperfectly perfect, ever-changing work of art. Echo this beauty within and around you. We can be presumptuous and misguided in our attempts to script and control life. Plan and prepare as we may, life has its own divine plan for us. When we choose to live and let live we exist organically, humbly and openly. We resist the exhausting urge to edit and neaten things, perfect and change things at our own expense. We let things be beautiful as they are — we allow ourselves to be beautiful as we are — and we learn to deeply trust and enjoy our path. And, without ambivalence or passivity, rather with respect for ourselves and living, we allow the proverbial ship of life to sail herself. We free energy we once spent unnecessarily fussing, intervening, controlling and striving for illusive perfection to focus on what truly matters. As it happens, we find ourselves available for the present moment — this very moment — the most important and only moment we truly have.

In Giving We Receive

We can all make a difference in the lives of others by being good, kind and compassionate people. It is understandable that we may feel rather overwhelmed in a world with many concerns vying for our loving attention. Thankfully, we can all transform our sadness and frustration into affirmative action in very meaningful ways. In doing so, we can channel our energy into practical initiatives drawing on our compassion for others, innate creativity and zest for life. How can we assist those in need within our families, communities and beyond? What gifts and talents might we have to offer that could be of helping, healing value to others? Even if we feel that we have nothing in particular to give, we must never underestimate the value of our loving presence: a listening ear, a smile or a hand to hold. Such humble offerings may be simple, yet true generosity of spirit has the power to turn lives around. Delightfully, giving of our love and care not only supports others, it imbues us with purpose and joy. Indeed, in the words of St Francis of Assissi, 'It is in giving that we receive.' By exploring initiatives close to home and further afield we will find opportunities to offer our time and care, even discovering inspiration to generate our very own wonderful ideas. As we turn our minds, hearts and hands to giving, we take part in much-needed healing and transformation here on earth.

Meditation

We meditate not to stop thinking, as the mind is designed to think and think it must. Rather, we meditate to slow and quieten our thoughts so that we may drink in the sensations of the present moment and connect with heaven at home within ourselves. Our meditations are not to be judged as good or bad, nor our approaches to meditation right or wrong. We may be sitting, lying, walking, ensconced in nature or taking in the essence of beauty. Our meditations may be brief or lengthy, structured or spontaneous. Most importantly, we feel a sense of reverence in our meditations — understanding them to be sacred moments in our lives. At best, our meditations encourage us to see that what we are seeking is already within us — peace, joy, balance and love. In light of this discovery, we learn to experience life without the stress of endlessly seeking more, instead becoming intimately attuned to all that we already possess — that which makes us inherently rich, whole and complete by nature.

As we transcend mental chatter and enter expanded states of awareness in meditation, we connect with our intuition, the voice of our spirit and our inner wisdom — the most precious guiding gift we possess. We also commune with our creativity — the powerhouse of our being. As the nourishment of meditation heightens our awareness, imbues us with energy and fills our cups, we find that we have so much more love and presence to pour into life and that, in return, life pours infinitely more love, peace and joy into us.

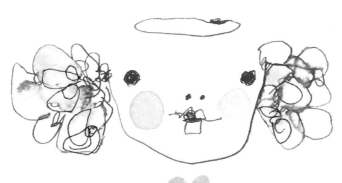

117

Treasured Moments

There are many ways to treasure a moment but the most important and powerful way is to be in it: to be aware of all the sensory nuances and pleasures of it — the sound, feel, taste, texture and subtle, vital energy of it. Not to be preoccupied with relaying or sharing it with others, not comparing it with any other moment, not eclipsing it with overwhelming expectations, but rather being present to the robust, fragile, sublime quality of what is the eternal now. We can all find ourselves missing the most beautiful moments of our lives while lost in thoughts of the past or the future, focusing on what we lack rather than all that we do have, or distracted by a virtual reality. What is happening in our real lives is happening sensorially, viscerally and dynamically, once in a lifetime. Indeed, as Doris Day sang, 'We'll have this moment forever, but never ever again.' As we learn to live in mindful and loving awareness of life with each new day, we see that every moment is calling us to treasure and savour it. May we learn to arrive where we are as life unfolds, celebrating the potent magic, richness, immediacy and beauty of our lives. Let us quite simply be right here, right now, and in this way discover our truest treasure — peace and joy in the present moment.

Spaciousness

We are blessed with wide open spaces on earth to revive, refresh and bring clarity to us. Wide open spaces have the power to clear our minds, humble us with their magnitude and gift us a fresher, more expansive perspective on life and living. When feeling overwhelmed or in need of mental roominess, there is nothing quite like spaciousness to free our minds. The visceral experience of freeing ourselves within expansive natural landscapes is transformative and profound. As we escape into the wild majesty of nature we can feel our breath return to us, our mind decluttering, and our experience of what we perceive as problematic or insurmountable in our lives diminish. We can always rely on nature to show us a balance of the light and shade of a life lived through all seasons.

In nature we see acceptance of things just as they are, resilience in the face of change, and a divine order and harmony of which we, too, are a part. When we complicate our realities with our thoughts, words and actions, we lose mental space. When we clutter our physical spaces with things, we lose the roominess we yearn to feel. Our things begin to own us, and our experience of lightness is somehow curtailed. Nature reminds us to just be, and to be here now. As we linger longer in the energy of the land, inner simplifying and decluttering take place, imbuing us with the peace, aliveness and clarity we naturally seek.

Declutter

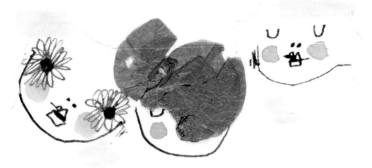

While many people live with very little, others live with great excess. This excess clutters our mental space as much as the physical spaces we inhabit. Our acquisitions take our energy in dollar value, storage, maintenance, time and care. The things we buy and own, in actuality, own us. Conversely, the things that enrich us most do not cost us a cent and energise us sustainably. A meaningful conversation, a walk in nature, a hug, a wild flower, a deep breath. Indeed, love cannot be bought, and neither can happiness. While procuring an object of our desire or affection may temporarily provide us a sense of happiness, we soon after find something else to covet and possess. Real joy is a state of being that is acquired not in things but in the quality of our thoughts and feelings. A calm, clear and peaceful mind is worth more than all the things we could ever buy or own. Understanding this makes decluttering a more compelling exercise. We can be sentimental while detached from 'things', making it easier to let go of that which we don't, or no longer, need. We can be sensitive and compassionate while releasing that which is not ours to carry, freeing our hearts and minds. Decluttering is conscious simplification. As we actively simplify our lives in every way, we find ourselves with room to move, see and feel clearly. In our decluttered world, our true, innermost selves are reflected back to us in the meaning, beauty and value of that which remains.

Be What You Are Looking For

We often wish, hope and pray for very important things such as peace, love, abundance and joy as if they are abstract, greater or external concepts, existing somewhere 'out there' in time and space. Alas, the greatest treasures we seek will not be bestowed upon us as gifts, but rather co-created by us as living, breathing, feeling beings in a constant dance with all there is. We cannot truly 'find' what we are looking for without 'be-ing' it first. It does not make sense to wish and hope for peace while living in disharmonious, cluttered or unthinking ways. Peace begins with us, and is cultivated in our peaceful thoughts, words and acts. Similarly, wishing and hoping for love whilst harbouring judgemental, unkind and fearful thoughts and beliefs about ourselves and others does not make sense. To 'find' love we must 'be' love — embodying it, choosing it and sharing it. Happiness eludes us too, when we disconnect from the energy of happiness, which, in its realest sense, is the rounded, all-encompassing spiritual energy of joy: our truest essence. Each one of us can experience joy by living mindfully, lovingly and gratefully, discovering true richness at spirit level. May we choose to be what we are looking for right now, and, in doing so, call off the search.

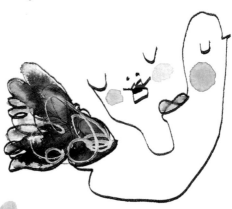

Taking Breaks

Taking breaks away from our daily lives and routines is essential for cultivating wellbeing — mind, body and soul. Rest and relaxation reset and rejuvenate us, and a change of scene naturally and necessarily changes our view. While our differing needs and desires will dictate our destinations and the pace at which we will travel, seeking out tranquil landscapes, calm, natural settings and full immersion in the eternal now, gifts a reprieve from what can accidentally become blinkered and braced daily living. We may find a special place we love and return to regularly, all the while keeping it as a sanctuary in our hearts and minds: a retreat to which our spirits may escape for relaxation in any moment we please. We may not have one place but rather many different places to which we can retreat, as we delight in exploring new terrain and possibilities for peace. The temptation may exist to keep running at our usual pace while away, but it is in quietude and stillness that we truly revive. While it is lovely to spend long stretches of time away if we are able to, even a single night away savoured mindfully can imbue us with the refreshment we seek. A rested field yields a bountiful crop. As we take time out in harmonious surroundings and disconnect even briefly from our daily reality, we find our senses awakened and our energy for life renewed.

Tears

'Heaven knows we need never
be ashamed of our tears' wrote
Charles Dickens. In our tears we
experience our humanity and it is in
experiencing our humanity that we
feel whole — alone and together.
In our joy and pain, in the face
of great loss or great beauty, we
can find ourselves moved to tears.
Our tears, often falling beyond our
control, can be healing and sublime.
Poet Robert Herrick described tears
as the noble language of our eyes —
that when we cannot find adequate
words for our feelings, or when we
feel beyond words, our tears speak
for us. We can be humbled by our
tears, even cleansed and refreshed
by them. Indeed, our tears work

for us in fascinating biochemical
ways, very much in keeping with our
remarkably intelligent human design.
Shedding tears can soothe and calm
us by activating our parasympathetic
nervous systems, relieve our pain
through the release of oxytocin,
elevate our mood through the
stimulation of endorphins, even
facilitate the release of toxins from
our bodies. Such inner processes may
explain why we cry, and why we
often feel much better afterwards.
'I was better after I had cried, than
before — more sorry, more aware
of my own ingratitude, more gentle.'
Dickens wrote on. To be sure, if
our tears help us to embrace our
sensitivity, feel gratitude and be
softened to the fullness of life and
love, may our tears flow.

Bodymind

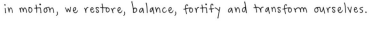

The mind follows the body and the body follows the mind. Our minds and bodies are constantly communicating with each other in a lifelong conversation determined, and forever eavesdropped upon, by our omniscient spirits. By design, our minds and bodies exist in complete collaboration. Our minds and bodies journey with us, moment to moment, determining the quality of our lives. Yet, we are not our bodies and we are not our minds — we are the intelligence synchronising the two. As we become more willing to harmonise our minds with our bodies, we naturally align our own rhythms with the rhythms of life. The result of cultivating 'bodymind' harmony is graceful living and the bliss of knowing equanimity — a state of calm composure. Meditation and meditative activities are very precious resources to help us unite our minds and bodies in conscious flow. Mindfulness in motion — gentle and strenuous alike, from tai-chi to qi-gong and dance — involves conscious movements in which our mind follows our breath and our breath is attuned to our movement. Practising mindfulness in motion, we restore, balance, fortify and transform ourselves.

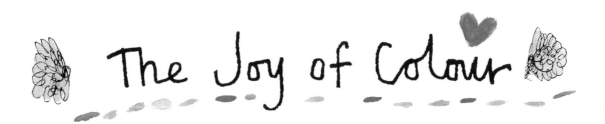

The Joy of Colour

A veritable kaleidoscope of colours paints our world with infinite beauty, miracles, moods and sensory delights. The majesty of iridescent flowers in full bloom; the wonder of creatures great and small; rainbow butterflies to pink flamingos; tropical fish to wild birds; the mesmerising and ever-changing palettes of sunrise and sunset; giddy blue sky between soft white clouds; the changing colours of an opal; the secret worlds within the pupils of our very own eyes — in these and endless other ways, the language of colour enchants and connects us, gifting us delightful pleasure and inspiration. Artist Paul Klee was so inspired by music that his colour palette and compositions have been described as 'painting music', as if they are translations of sound into line and colour. The Japanese art of shinrin-yoku ('forest bathing') is effective partly thanks to the special ability of the colour green to soothe and relax our minds. We can enter interior spaces painted in different colours to notice our moods change, from the warm embrace of pink to the joy of yellow and the quiet bliss of soft blue. Wearing different colours and tones has the power to change our state of mind and being, too, from confident, resplendent red to crisp, pure and peaceful white. Remarkably, while there is a studied and documented psychology of colour, we all respond uniquely to the stimulus and energy of different colours. As ever, exploring and celebrating our varied tastes makes life all the more compelling and wonderful. The more appreciative and aware we become of beauty on earth, the more colours speak to us. As we connect with colours in our own unique, mindful and creative ways, we tap into endless inspiration — a therapeutic, generous and joyous gift in daily life.

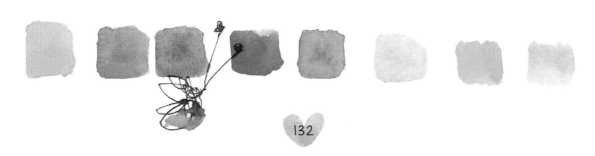

Sound

In flow, we enter an expanded state of awareness in which we are opened to the limitless, heavenly and creative energy of life. This creative energy is available to all of us. It dwells within and around us, ready and waiting to nourish, enrich and revitalise us completely. We enter flow states by dropping down from our busy minds to spirit level via our sensing, feeling bodies. In flow, we may lose our sense of time, and of ourselves, completely. Indeed, a new spaciousness opens up to us when we enter flow — a space beyond perfectionism, striving or control. A realm in which we loosen into blissful surrender. A realm in which we are humbled and exhilarated. In flow, we experience ourselves as instruments of creative energy, expanding and flourishing in unbridled ways that elevate our spirits and empower us profoundly. We may be in flow running, drawing, meditating, playing music — whatever activity it is into which we may truly, deeply sink. Melting into flow beyond time and space, we become imbued with the positively magical charge of life.

Effort

Making sincere effort in life is fundamental to our health and happiness. Our willingness to make effort determines our life story, our sense of satisfaction, and our connection to meaning, purpose and contribution in this life. A spider builds its web in the elements with tremendous precision and care, irrespective of the elements' propensity to destabilise it, or the possibility of human touch to destroy it. Building webs, be they vulnerable and fragile, is part of the spider's life force and design. In a world that can seem challenging and overwhelming, and in which we may perceive our efforts to be feeble or of little consequence, we must continue to choose effort over apathy — contribution and faith in life over inactivity and resignation. In the words of playwright Tennessee Williams, 'Make voyages! – Attempt them! – there's nothing else ...' Indeed, we must endeavour and aim high, believing in the value, joy and reward of endeavouring itself. This way we may allow the outcome, destination or reward of our work to be the icing on our proverbial cake of life — and effort itself our greatest joy.

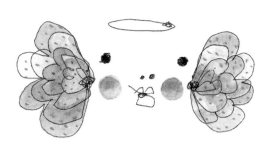

Alone and Together

It is very natural that we exist alone and together, respecting our need for connection as much as our need for quietude and solitude in this life. While it may be compelling to define ourselves as introverts or extroverts, the truth is that we all possess both inclinations — inclinations that come to the fore for us contextually. Certain moods, reasons, circumstances or seasons call us within to be with ourselves: to quieten down, reflect, hear our inner voice and notice the spaciousness and freedom of a nurtured inner world. Other moments call us to reach out to one another — talking, playing, singing, dancing and having fun in harmony. All parts of ourselves must be welcome. All parts of ourselves belong to our whole selves. Flexibility and loving acceptance of ourselves as we constantly move, grow and change gifts us a balanced life: a rich life savoured alone and together.

Letting Go

The past can be full of overwhelming grief, loss and sadness. We may feel burdened by difficult feelings, memories, even regrets and 'what-ifs' of all kinds. We have a choice to dwell in the past — but only in our minds. We have no real choice to go back in time, as the past no longer exists. It has gone. Existing in the present while dwelling in the past causes us great tension, fatigue and pain, as we effectively find ourselves in no time at all. The past is over and the future is not yet here. Indeed, actually 'living' in the past is an option unavailable to us, and, as such, will unendingly frustrate, compromise and unbalance us with possibilities for even greater unhappiness. While we may seek solace in the past — in familiarity, in reminiscing, or even finding comfort in our pain — in truly choosing to live, we must be here now. Being here now necessarily involves letting go of the past, a time that we can no longer have, be, change or live. Being here now necessarily means choosing to see what we do and can have, what we wish and dream to have, and that includes happiness. The present moment offers us the chance to truly be, and to begin again. To take a breath and start now. The present moment is always the most powerful moment we have, brimming with potential, promise and deep peace. Just a moment of courage allows us to begin letting go. As we continue to let go, gently and surely surrendering any old doubts and fears, we find great, often unexpected strength within us. All we must then do is humbly allow life to carry us, refreshing, delighting and nourishing us with its own magical plan.

Go Your Own Way

'It is time that we steered by the stars, not by the lights of each passing ship', stated US military general Omar Bradley. When we realise that being ourselves brings us the greatest peace and joy imaginable, and that trying to be anyone other than ourselves causes us a whole range of terribly uncomfortable and dissatisfying experiences, we find infinite courage and inspiration to chart our very own course. Going our own way is best done in peace, joy and integrity rather than carried out as an act of rebellion. Even if going our own way involves stepping out from the crowd, surprising and disappointing others, or subverting preconceived ideas or plans, we are best to go about our own courses in calm, self-assured, respectful ways. Going our own way means that we accept ourselves, liberate ourselves to live our dreams, express our individuality and make conscious choices in support of our learning, growing and flourishing in this life. Our lives are not performances, but nor are they dress rehearsals. No one else can learn our lessons or write our stories for us. We must travel our own paths and co-create our own realities in harmony with what we ultimately find to be the ever-supportive energy of life. What we see and believe for ourselves, we become. What we envision for our lives, we experience. We are not limited by our past, by others' behaviours, nor by others' opinions or expectations of us. Our lives are determined by the personal energy we bring to them. May we go our own ways, taking responsibility for cultivating positivity, making sincere effort, and living life in gratitude.

Reaching Out

While cultivating courage fortifies us, we needn't be stoic at our own expense. We needn't and indeed mustn't deny our very real needs for support, love and care. There is a reason why kin and community structures have governed humanity since time immemorial — we were not created to face life alone. An epidemic of loneliness is afflicting our planet, but we have the power to transform it by actualising meaningful connections with others. There is a beautiful balance we can strike between taking responsibility for ourselves — knowing ourselves, nurturing ourselves and extending ourselves to grow — and reaching out to others when needed. As we reach out in connection, we honour others' wisdom and strength. We unite in support of one another and in a shared experience of humanity. There is tremendous courage in humility and vulnerability.

We must sometimes admit and accept that we cannot handle it all; that some things are not meant for us; and that we may not have all the answers we seek. Living truthfully and openly in this way, we set a powerful example for others to reach out and connect sincerely, too. There will be moments we need practical or emotional support, a different opinion or new perspective. Moments we yearn for light conversation, a holding hand, a listening ear or time spent in gentle company. It is important to realise that our internal needs may not always be intuited, even by the ones we know and love the most. As such, it becomes very important to speak our hearts and minds, inviting ourselves to be understood. Reaching out is about connection. May we be approachable people ready to care for others while opening ourselves to being loved and supported at every turn, too.

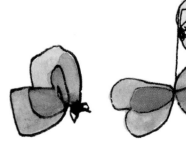

Be the Change

We can expend a tremendous amount of our vital energy trying to make sense of senselessness on earth. While our precious personal energy has profound and potent purpose in creativity and love, we can inadvertently find ourselves in low-frequency thinking — stuck in the very energies that created the problems we seek to reconcile in our hearts and minds. To preserve our vital energy and put it to best use, we must think and aim higher. We must suspend our disbelief, transcend our mental clutter, and realign ourselves fervently and actively with peace and joy. Our collective wellbeing as one humanity must shape our vision, alongside our faith in prevailing goodness and in miracles of all kinds. Living slowly, simply, gently and kindly, with integrity and with a genuine desire to contribute to a greater good, nourishes, anchors and connects us all. Albert Einstein is credited with the assertion that: 'We cannot solve our problems with the same thinking we used when we created them.' Indeed, many problems we face in today's world derive from fear, acquisitiveness at the expense of others, spiritual poverty, and a sense of separateness that undermines our shared humanity. We must instead think and lead with truly united, empowered and compassionate hearts and minds. In this way, we may tap into a wellspring of renewable positive energy — love — and become the change we wish to see in our world.

No More, No Less

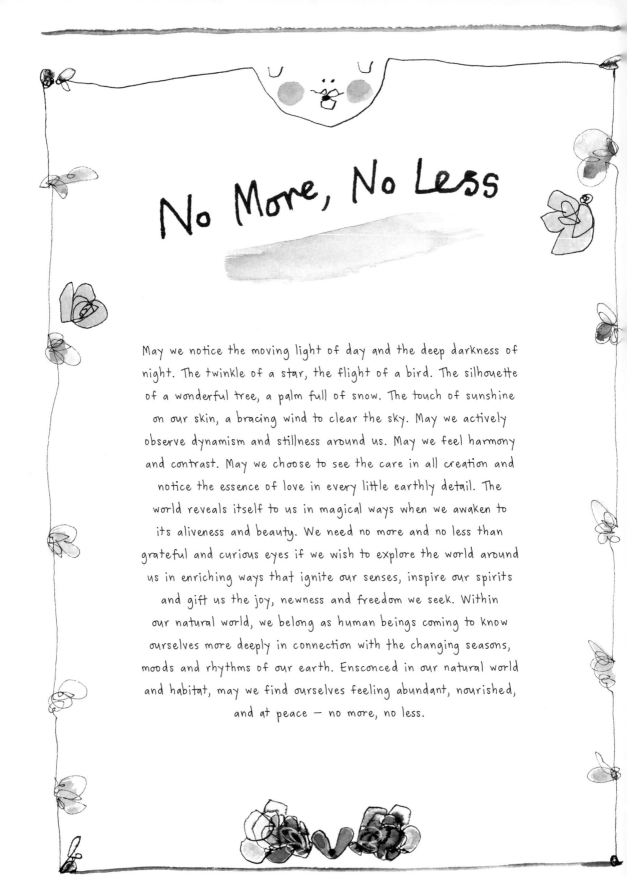

May we notice the moving light of day and the deep darkness of night. The twinkle of a star, the flight of a bird. The silhouette of a wonderful tree, a palm full of snow. The touch of sunshine on our skin, a bracing wind to clear the sky. May we actively observe dynamism and stillness around us. May we feel harmony and contrast. May we choose to see the care in all creation and notice the essence of love in every little earthly detail. The world reveals itself to us in magical ways when we awaken to its aliveness and beauty. We need no more and no less than grateful and curious eyes if we wish to explore the world around us in enriching ways that ignite our senses, inspire our spirits and gift us the joy, newness and freedom we seek. Within our natural world, we belong as human beings coming to know ourselves more deeply in connection with the changing seasons, moods and rhythms of our earth. Ensconced in our natural world and habitat, may we find ourselves feeling abundant, nourished, and at peace — no more, no less.

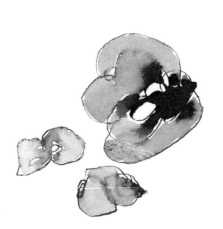

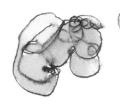

Triumphant

Naturalist Ralph Waldo Emerson wrote that the earth laughs in flowers. It teaches in flowers, too. Flowers do not bloom in a hierarchy of greatness; indeed weeds flourish proudly amongst flowers, not knowing or caring that they may be referred to as weeds or considered any less than their garden bed-fellows. As it happens, a weed in one place may be considered a flower in another and, moreover, admirable and beautiful in its own right, and also in the eyes of beholders. Rain, sun, wind and snow do not discriminate and embrace each flower the same as the seasons change. Flowers do not compete, nor are they self-conscious or withholding; rather, they are often seen to flourish triumphantly, even in the most unexpected and life-affirming ways. Notice a tiny daisy growing up between the concrete of the pavement. Watch you don't step on it! ... See little tendrils of fig or ivy crawling through windows and tickling walls from the outside in. See tiny green shoots springing up after a bushfire has passed through, triumphantly regenerating as signs of life prevailing. Be inspired to bloom your way, wherever you are. Indeed, we must bloom triumphantly where we are and, just as little seeds fly into the wind spreading life, let our effort and aliveness grow the promise of joy.

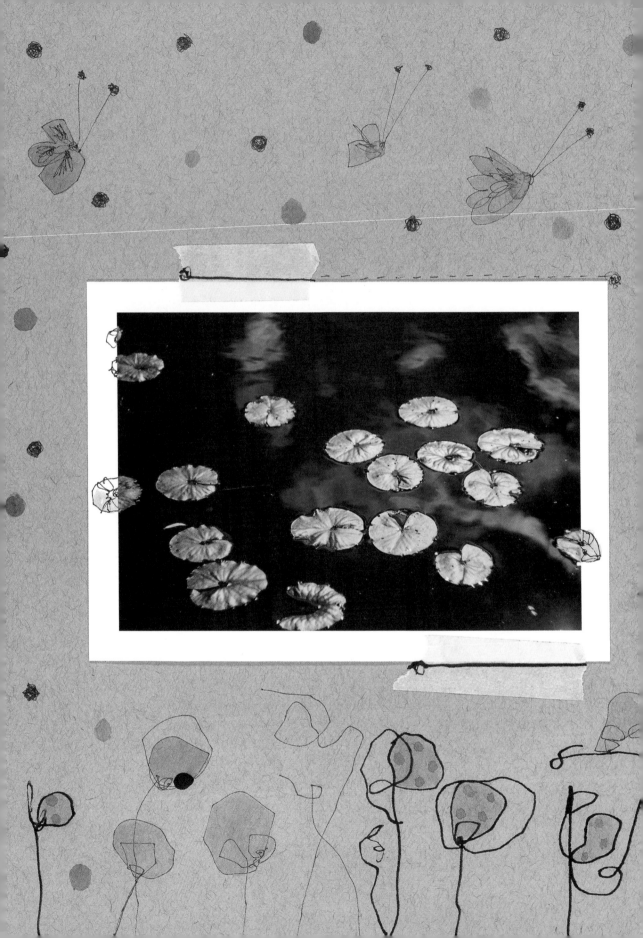

What Lies Beneath

When light shines upon the darkness of a pond, that which lies beneath its smooth, glossy surface is revealed. What may have appeared to be rather still and quiet is, in fact, brimming with the energy of life. We may see wonderful, tangled root systems, floating organic matter, and various aquatic life going about its business. When clouds or darkness gather above the very same water, the surface of the pond appears opaque again. Its mysterious depths and wonders — the magical inner world of the pond — are suddenly invisible to us. In effect, what we are seeing is an incomplete picture, the completion of which is made possible by light. In remarkable similarity, and in the light of our own mindful awareness, we come to discover that there is so much to see, love and explore within ourselves. Choosing to live mindfully, we expand our experience of ourselves and life to depths well beyond surface level. As we welcome light to shine upon and permeate us completely, we naturally glow in the full splendour of our aliveness. We come to see and treasure all our layers, shadows, vulnerabilities and secret pleasures, most especially the transformative treasures that lie beneath our surface — beneath that which we and others may see with eyes alone. Illuminated, we experience ourselves as nuanced, magical and complete by nature: just as we are.

revelation

A secret, subtle world exists to enchant, inspire and enliven us with its poetry: a magical world in which we cannot and are not meant to know everything; in which imagination is very precious and essential; and in which material and dream worlds intertwine. Not all things give themselves away easily. Certain people, concepts, plans and dreams can be quite elusive — even enigmatic. They can show themselves surreptitiously, if at all. They can require particular gentleness and respect, quietude and a careful approach. They can require less presumption and more time and space to be seen. Eluding precise definition or description, even understanding, such subtle things invite us to be with them humbly and openly. In time, wonderful mysteries may reveal themselves to us, just as mist will rise over a landscape and reveal what lies beneath — quietly, and at its own pace, not at any request or whim of our own. Many aspects of modern life are quite unsubtle, overt and brash. We can be impatient, demanding, and very literal, forgetting grace and the charms of mystery. Sit gently with subtler things. Let their withholding and mystery delight you, their dance of revelation enchant.

Seasons

Ancient Greek philosopher Heraclitus wrote that we cannot step in the same river twice as it is not the same river and we are not the same people. Indeed, the wisdom and experience we accrue over time, the ups and downs we traverse, the relationships that grow and change us, the passions we cultivate and the dreams we follow see us shift and change in profound ways through the various seasons of our lives. All the while, living in sincerity and integrity as we grow and change, our roots take more deeply into the soil to ground and fortify us. By choosing self-respect, patience and faith through our shifting seasons, we can let go of unnecessary judgement and relax into the true joy of transformation. It is life-affirming to watch how trees simply let go of their old leaves, by nature, making way for new growth. We must make it within our nature to let go, too: to make room for new life, new possibilities, new learning and new bliss in our lives. We are not to hold ourselves accountable, nor be held accountable, to being a particular way we used to be at some other place or at some other time. Our lives inevitably require mindful pruning as we shift and change, meaning that some ideas, structures, relationships or beliefs will call for release. To live in peace, we must trust that all things truly meant for us will stay and flourish with and within us over time, while those things not meant for us will change with the seasons, as the seasons must, and do, change. Transforming with faith in gratitude for life, we find we have nothing to lose and everything to gain.

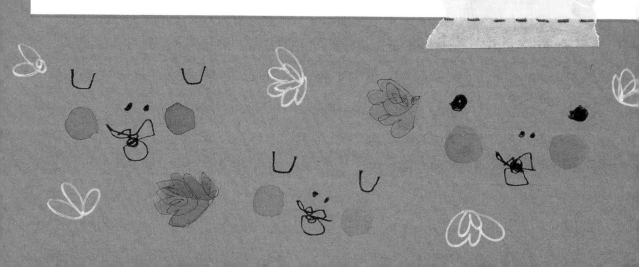

Ancient Landscapes

Moments spent in the depth and breadth of nature's splendour dwarf, mesmerise and bedazzle us. We can even find our spirits catapulted back in time, or feel the wonderful, secret stories of the planet upon which we live. Ancient landscapes brim with the energy of times gone by and of other life on earth. See textured rock faces where ocean waves once washed to shore. Notice trees once burnt by fire growing again and again. Hear the footsteps of dinosaurs, or ponder the hidden fossils of creatures great and small. Admire how rivers have run over rocks, forming their wonderful, curvaceous shapes. Notice how the kiss of the sun has lightened and brightened the face of the earth. There is nothing like the sheer scale and magnificence of nature to speak to our own aliveness and humble us with its unspeakable power. It is no wonder that within ancient landscapes we can find ourselves experiencing deep, enduring healing. The solidity and peace of our living, breathing earth — the intensity and wonder of nature — restores our senses, encouraging us to explore aspects of timelessness, beauty and mystery within ourselves. Energised by our earth, we connect with ourselves as part of nature. We honour our past, harmonise with our present, and feel inspired to care deeply for all we are gifted as custodians of this heavenly earth.

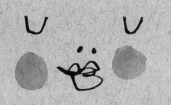

Music

Human beings have forever made and been moved
by music. Studies in sound reveal its quantifiably
stimulating and healing effects upon us, even more deeply
illuminating the magical potency of music in our lives. Music
touches us — brings us to life, brings back memories, makes us
dance, sing, laugh and cry — makes us feel something. And, in
feeling something, we are changed. Indeed, we can change the way we
feel by changing the music we listen to, and this is due to the way music
speaks to us at an energetic, cellular level. While lyrics may resonate with
us at thought level, sound is a phenomenon experienced subconsciously
through tones and frequencies read by our ears, translated by our minds
and moved through our bodies as energy — a completely visceral experience.
Indeed, we intuitively choose gentle music to settle and comfort ourselves,
more stimulating music to feel elevated and energised. We intuitively
choose music to either match or to consciously shift our mood. Respecting
music in mindful ways, we begin to acknowledge it as a very precious
companion on our emotional landscape — a companion to be treasured
with care. Appreciating the truly transformative, experiential nature
of music, we may consciously activate its power and presence in our
days, curating personal soundtracks to our unique lives. Tailor-
making playlists to meet our needs and desires throughout the
day, we can collaborate with music in wonderful ways: enhancing
our state of being, ritualising certain parts of life, welcoming
wakefulness, concentration or rest, even dipping into meditation.
And, in a secret world of its very own, beyond definition or
explanation, time or space, the magic of music will forever dwell,
ready to move us. Heinrich Heine is credited with the statement
that where words leave off, music begins.

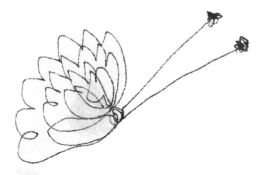
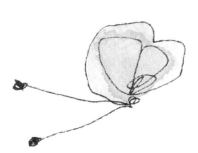

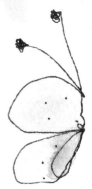
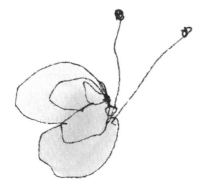
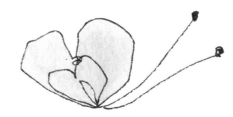

Tea Ceremony

'"After all," Anne had said to Marilla once, "I believe the nicest and sweetest days are not those on which anything very splendid or wonderful or exciting happens but just those that bring simple little pleasures, following one another softly, like pearls slipping off a string."' wrote Lucy Maude Montgomery in 'Anne of Avonlea'. Indeed, the little pleasure of tea drinking, a simple daily delight, is one such sweet, wonderful thing that, with a little time and care, may become a beautiful and cherished ritual. By drawing upon the finest teacups and teapot we can procure, sourcing a tea blend we adore, taking time to brew our tea, set the scene and add delectable, edible morsels to our tea tray if desired, we may mindfully create our own little tea ceremony — a moment in the day to softly, sweetly savour one of the littlest but greatest pleasures of life. Tea ceremonies need not be savoured in company to be enjoyed. Tea for one is occasion enough.

In Japanese culture tea ceremonies are spectacular, elaborate and last for many hours. Ceremonial utensils are handled in special ways, guests participate as if in prayer, and the scene is set to perfection. May we draw inspiration from such reverence, and relish the elevation of a simple act into a heavenly pleasure.

The School of Life

Life is a learning experience. When we look at life as such, we release the need to know things or to be right all the time, instead softening into a journey of discovery in which we are open, humble and flexible. We are able to take ourselves less seriously, laugh more freely, feel more comfortable to ask questions, and seek help when needed. We also find great joy in self-reflection, accountability and personal growth. If we choose to embrace our learning in the school of life, we can observe ourselves compassionately and without judgement, seeing that when we know better, we do better. Moments in which we could have chosen differently present themselves to us as lessons, and areas of our lives in which we wish to see positive change — presenting to us in the form of discomfort, stress or strain — call very clearly for our love, time and care. We begin to see a benevolent inner intelligence that always wishes to help us on our way, and we realise that the only prerequisite for advancing on our course is willingness. We are never too early or too late for class as the school of life is timeless — its magical door is always open.

Make a Wish

There is a saying that a goal without a plan is just a wish. Indeed, to realise our goals and dreams requires more than just wishful thinking. Living each day as if in our dreams awake is a proactive, creative and faithful collaboration with life. It is also a way of being that allows us to feel empowered and enchanted as we travel our paths. Life's grand plan has an intelligence of its very own and at certain times, this intelligence can seem counter to our own thoughts and desires, plans and visions. Choosing to live joyously and faithfully — even and especially in the face of twists and turns that may seem at odds with our own agendas — we become a creative part of making our dreams come true in the highest, most remarkable and unexpected ways.

As we do our very best and then surrender our expectations, we allow the power of love to work its magic in our lives. Our plan must then be to merge with life by loving and trusting it. In doing so, we ultimately find ourselves wish-less. We find that the conditions for happiness dwell within us and are ours to nurture. In a world of wanting, we are wise to see that the things we may take for granted can be the stuff of others' greatest dreams. Water to drink, a dive into the ocean, sun on our skin, the ability to walk, talk or travel. Next time we come to set a goal, devise a plan or make a wish, perhaps we can add a prayer to it too — a prayer of thanks for all that we do have, and for all the good that is yet to come. Practising gratitude as we dream on, we find life unfolding in deeply rewarding, wonderful ways.

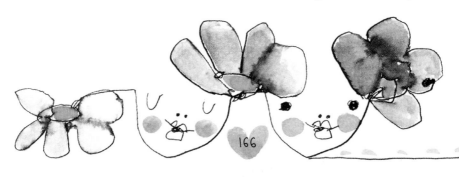

The Tree of Life

May we pay our respects to the strength, beauty, comfort and shelter of trees. Many trees with whom we share our planet are far older and wiser than we are. As such, they are to be shown true love and care — to be admired and protected, nurtured and planted. May we give thanks for the way trees oxygenate our planet, protect us from the elements, create unique visions of gorgeousness around us, make homes for creatures of so many kinds, keep our secrets, bear wonderful fruit and flowers, and quietly, unassumingly, watch over us. Beginning as seeds, taking tiny shoots, then flourishing — some to tremendous heights — trees teach us that, as in singer-songwriter Paul Kelly's famous song, from little things, big things grow. As we watch trees weather rain, hail, storm and sunshine we see the depth of their roots. As seasons change and certain trees lose their leaves in a splendid show, naked over winter and coming to life again in springtime, we see nature in harmonic intelligence with the earth's seasons. Trees are symbols of new life, growth, transformation and resilience. In their divine, omniscient way, trees call us to embrace our own aliveness in gifting us their very own.

Speechless

There are truly spellbinding places on earth, places so unbelievably sublime that they stir our spirits to tears of gratitude and wonder. Our resplendent earth — the place we are so privileged to call home — brims with sensory delights through which we may commune with the awe-inspiring, potent energy of life — of creation and higher love. Breathtaking landscapes can render us speechless. There are quite simply no words for them. Indeed, profound, silent contemplation seems only appropriate in such contexts: places in which speech seems inadequate, even irreverent. In her exquisite piece of nature writing, The Living Mountain, Nan Shepherd writes of reverently experiencing nature and sharing its exquisiteness in company. 'The perfect hill companion,' she writes, 'is the one whose identity is for the time being merged in that of the mountains, as you feel your own to be. Then such speech as arises is part of a common life and cannot be alien. To "make conversation", however, is ruinous, to speak may be superfluous.' Watch sunrises and sunsets colour the sky. Notice shorelines curve and zigzag, creating wonderful patterns in shifting tides. See the sun dance over undulating hills and listen as the wind tickles long grasses. Watch the earth play in a symphony of quiet order and perfection, humbly surrendering yourself into the spellbinding energy of sublimity. In such moments of bliss beyond words, writes Shepherd, '... to listen is better than to speak.'

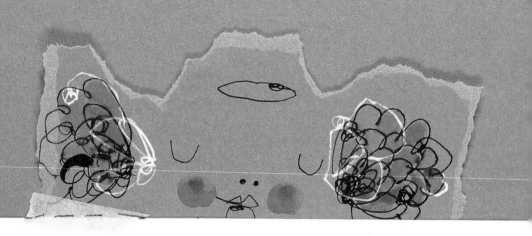

Nourishing Wilderness

The depth of a forest has the power to nourish us very deeply. In Japanese culture, shinrin-yoku or 'forest bathing' is celebrated as a healing art. Understood to work on the mind and body in rejuvenating and fortifying ways, it is also used in convalescence as therapy for people who have been unwell to regain their energy for life, and in the treatment of stress, anxiety and depression. The vivid, textural, all-encompassing visceral immersion of the forest atmosphere positively cocoons us. Between the forest floor and canopy, we are at one with nature. With reverence for a forest, we can merge with it — become part of it. And, as we move through its precious, wild spaces, we see the heartening, wandering magic of life sprawling free — untouched. A world of tangled vines, dappled light, wispy ferns and braided roots. A world in compelling contrast to the organisation and order of the built, urban environments in which most of us dwell. As we quieten down, we begin to hear the hum of insects and the song of birds. Gently, gently as we go, other creatures may feel comfortable and safe enough to cross our paths. In the forest, there is no distraction, hurry or comparison. Things grow yet are forever complete. And, within it, the new world slips away. Peace embraces us, and the wisdom of nature works with and within us in very real, quantifiable ways. Our minds, our physical and emotional hearts — all our cells are touched and changed. Forest bathing helps us to experience how to be here now. The majestic aliveness and ancient splendour of wilderness teaches us about timelessness, careful seeing and imperfect perfection. May we sensitively, gracefully enter our earthly forests at every opportunity.

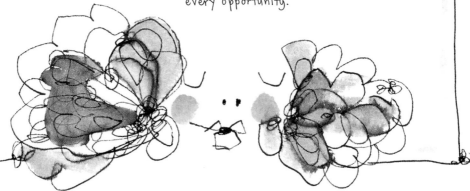

The Way Appears

While there is merit in being prepared, setting goals and having a destination in mind, it would be presumptuous of us to believe that our life journeys are completely within our control. Unscripted, unexpected developments of all kinds can create both wonderful and trying diversions on the paths we might have envisaged for ourselves. Indeed, the ship of life sails herself and we are implored to live fully and faithfully, letting her do so. When we journey fearfully and begrudgingly, experiencing our lives as problems to be solved, life mirrors our attitude back to us in all manner of unwanted experiences and states of being, confirming our negative beliefs and perpetuating our unhappiness. Conversely, when we surrender to the unknown and move through life with humility and positivity, we magnetise joyous and life-affirming experiences toward us, enhancing and illuminating our lives. When we see and believe that life is on our side and we live as such, we welcome peace and bliss into each moment. We needn't always know, nor can we ever truly know, exactly where we are going next — where we will be in five years' or even five days' time — but we can live courageously and gratefully right here and now. One step at a time is more than enough, even and especially during difficult times in which we cannot quite see our path forward. In the words of Sufi mystic Rumi, 'As you start to walk on the way, the way appears.'

The Play of Time

We all have the same number of hours in each day, and yet time is always what we make it. Our experience of time is in great part shaped by our emotional relationship with it. Some days we are focused and productive, achieving great things and sensing true satisfaction at the end of the day. With mindful attention, we find that on such days we are in tune with positive self-talk and a higher mood. Other days, we feel as if we have achieved very little with our time. On such days, we are invariably experiencing lower moods and less kinetic energy within. Time might have dragged or escaped us. Observe how time can fly when you are having fun, or move at glacial speed when you feel unstimulated. Indeed, time is a fascinating illusion that physicists can prove to be malleable, not linear, as we generally conceive it to be. Albert Einstein referred to the past, present and future as arbitrary, albeit very stubborn, constructs by which our lives are governed.

Human beings created a vernacular for time — seconds, minutes, hours, days, years, decades, centuries — as a shared, functional language. As language shapes our experience, we all learn to experience time in measurements, accepting these human constructs as givens. Yet we live in an extraordinarily magical and mysterious world — an enigmatic world that is meant to bedazzle us, and that works above and beyond any human structures of organisation. What if we were to allow ourselves to suspend all that we think we know about time and enter a more creative, far less rigid relationship with it, experimenting with our emotional experience of time in open and intimate ways? What if we were to make time work for us, expanding and contracting it with our consciousness? You may ask yourself, what would you like to do with your time? And, how would you like time to feel? As we become more attuned to ourselves and the mysteries of being, our experience of life becomes intelligent play and time is like putty in our hands.

Coming Home

The feeling of coming home, like an embrace, can bring us the most sublime comfort and relief, especially at the end of a big day or long journey. The simple pleasures of home offer themselves to us without pretence or pride, humbly and familiarly, as a balm for our spirits. At home where our hearts dwell, where we may be completely ourselves, we can nestle in and gather our thoughts and feelings. We may integrate the events of a day or a lifetime, care for ourselves, each other, our plants and our pets, and feel ensconced in an atmosphere of our own creation. In the curation and care of our homes, we are wise to remember that we are actively creating sacred spaces — our own little heavens and private sanctuaries. When we respect and nurture our homes, we sense our love reflected back to us by way of deep peace and comfort. As we take care of our outer spaces, each homecoming provides the inner calm and joy we seek. We may already live in our dream home or we may be in a place that feels temporary. Irrespective of our circumstances, we must love and care for the place we call home, right now. We mustn't delay or withhold our love for home; we must dwell in it. Being gracious in the present, we not only begin to make the very best of all that we have, we expedite the realisation of our innermost dreams. With reverence and care, our homes become restorative havens for truly peaceful, joyous living.

Feet Up

The most decadent luxuries in life are usually the simplest. While we might turn our minds to more grandiose visions of indulgence, the littlest, humblest pleasures are invariably the ones to bring us the most exquisite peace and joy. Taking time to honour our need for quietude and rest, be that a brief moment or a whole afternoon's repose, lets our minds and bodies know that we love them. The loving dynamic we can cultivate in our relationship with ourselves — one of thankfulness and thoughtfulness — sets the tone for a beautiful and relaxing life. Rather than deny ourselves quietude and little luxuries of all kinds, never stopping to pause, we can actively make, see and savour moments for essential self-care each day. Indeed, self-care is not selfish or self-indulgent, it is a necessary foundation for our personal wellbeing — the sustainable energy we possess to carry us through our days. We can all make simple but decadent and delicious moments in our day, from putting our feet up to slipping into bed for a little siesta, from a quiet cup of tea to a slow bath or little meditation. As we show ourselves the love and respect we by nature deserve, we reaffirm to ourselves day by day that inner peace and joy matter, and that we are being deservedly treasured.

Enchantment

It has been suggested that Albert Einstein thought that there are two ways we can experience life: as if nothing is a miracle, and as if everything is. Opening ourselves to the ever-presence of life's magic allows us to feel perpetual enchantment. Living with awareness of ourselves as miracles amongst miracles, we nourish our imaginations, replenish our wellsprings of creativity and heighten our awareness of our own divinity: divinity we embody quite simply by virtue of our aliveness. We are part of all there is. Our own miraculous aliveness is echoed back to us in the beauty of our living, breathing natural world. As we explore ourselves and our earth, experiencing places, spaces and feelings within and around us, we awaken to the indescribable deliciousness and mysteriousness of life. How could such ever-changing perfection and natural order about us have come into being? How is it that we, in our careful design, interact with our surrounding environments in vital and complete symbiosis?

Mirrored in nature's ever-changing states and seasons are our own sensory landscapes and chapters of life. Appreciation for such details nourishes our hearts and enlivens our spirits. Komorebi is the Japanese word for the sunlight that filters through the leaves of trees. Like other sublime visions worthy of our mindfulness and appreciation, komorebi is one of countless miracles to savour as we go gratefully about our days — eyes and hearts open to enchantment, and spirits attuned to the wonder of living.

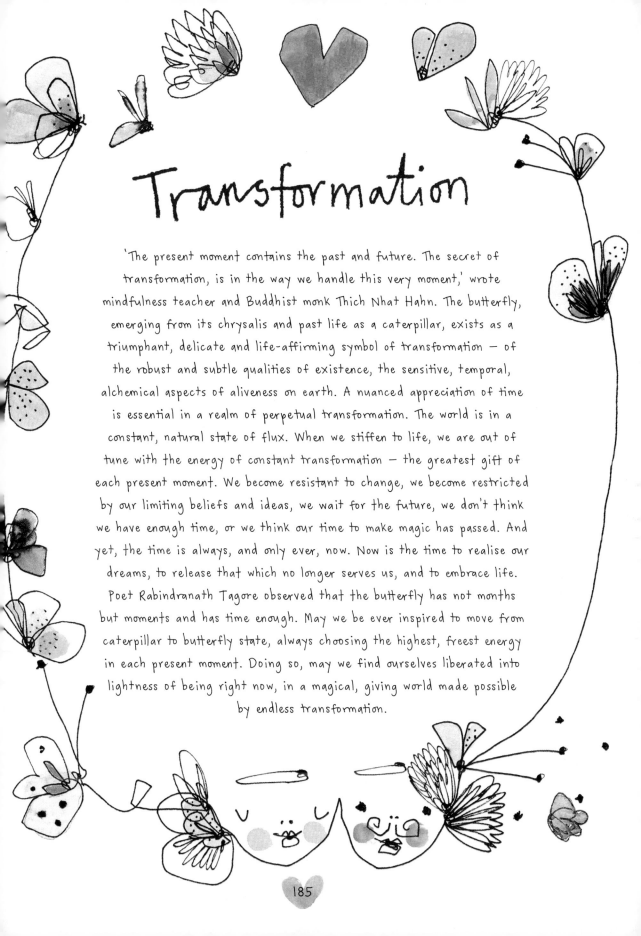

Transformation

'The present moment contains the past and future. The secret of transformation, is in the way we handle this very moment,' wrote mindfulness teacher and Buddhist monk Thich Nhat Hahn. The butterfly, emerging from its chrysalis and past life as a caterpillar, exists as a triumphant, delicate and life-affirming symbol of transformation — of the robust and subtle qualities of existence, the sensitive, temporal, alchemical aspects of aliveness on earth. A nuanced appreciation of time is essential in a realm of perpetual transformation. The world is in a constant, natural state of flux. When we stiffen to life, we are out of tune with the energy of constant transformation — the greatest gift of each present moment. We become resistant to change, we become restricted by our limiting beliefs and ideas, we wait for the future, we don't think we have enough time, or we think our time to make magic has passed. And yet, the time is always, and only ever, now. Now is the time to realise our dreams, to release that which no longer serves us, and to embrace life. Poet Rabindranath Tagore observed that the butterfly has not months but moments and has time enough. May we be ever inspired to move from caterpillar to butterfly state, always choosing the highest, freest energy in each present moment. Doing so, may we find ourselves liberated into lightness of being right now, in a magical, giving world made possible by endless transformation.

Journey On

New adventures, new delights and new choices constantly await us. We never know what might be around the corner, but we can be sure that our days will be enriching when we choose to live in love, joy and gratitude. Journeying on faithfully, and with an awareness of perpetual magic in the air, we may live our dreams awake. Journeying on, we must commit to creating our own mobile worlds in which to move and blossom — tender, beautiful inner worlds nurtured by our thoughts, self-talk and self-care. And, as best as we can, we must seek, protect and create beauty around us. Such an approach to life provides endless balm for our senses and spirits, gifting us strength, comfort and inspiration. Indeed, when feeling world-weary, at a crossroads and overwhelmed, or walking a dissatisfying, lacklustre path, it is simply time to honour ourselves, reaffirm the joyous purpose of our journey, and realign with true love and gratitude for life. As Dolly Parton suggested, if you don't like the path you are walking, pave a new one. In paving any new path, our spirits call us to be flexible and free — never holding on to old ideas and stifling limitations, but rather traversing fresh, bright and new ground as we evolve into our truest, highest selves.

Dearest You,

Brimming with promise and crafted from infinite potential, each present moment empowers us to let go and welcome new life. This constant process of refreshment and renewal gifts us endless chances to celebrate the magic of being and embrace ourselves as we grow and change. The all-powerful meeting place of our past and future is here and now. The past is no longer within our hands and the future is not yet ours to touch. The present moment is our greatest — and only — point of transformation.

Empowered by understanding the potency and power of the present moment, we are naturally compelled to dive deeply into all that we are and do. We understand that life is ours to live, we learn to respect the privilege of our aliveness, and we commit to making each moment matter.

Grateful, open-minded and open-hearted, we awaken to life as a magical experience. Sharpening our faculties we heighten our powers of observation and enliven our senses. Living this way, life becomes a waking dream — our own work of art.

Life calls us to join in co-creative partnership with it. We cannot wait for life to touch and move us; we must touch life, and willingly move with life, in order to accept the gift of our existence: our greatest gift. We needn't search far and wide for answers to even the most complicated of existential questions. The answer is simple, one and the same — to live in love with life is our reason for being. As we love and appreciate life, moment to moment, we are imbued with constant, renewable and vital energy. We sense deep satisfaction, we see the good and beauty in things, and we translate inspiration into creativity.

In a patchwork woven of light and dark threads, across landscapes rolling and jagged, upon seas smooth and wild alike, we are always at home within the energy of life. The constant flux of life ensures that nothing stays the same forever. Highs and lows create necessary texture in our lives, just as no beautiful symphony could ever be monotonal. The contrasts and challenges we

navigate teach and enrich us, growing us and shaping our character. We are not the same people from one moment to the next — we are forever changing. When we know better, we do better. When we learn to see, we see more. This is an ever-evolving process of opening up — of deepening into ourselves and life.

In the flow of life, we mustn't rely on the past to dictate our future; we must create afresh. We are not beholden to old ways of seeing or being — quite the contrary, we are constantly being invited to elevate the way we see things and the way we are by virtue of the dynamism and renewal of each present moment. As one present moment flows naturally into another, and as we inhale and exhale, we are reminded to let go, live and let live.

Accepting our invitation into the richness of life, we are fortified and inspired. In flow with life, we notice ourselves emerging like rainbows emerge after storms — even dancing in the sun showers of our lives. Joyously surrendering to loving and trusting

in life, we are strengthened and nourished to create our realities from a place of humility and freedom, gratitude and peace. From such a place, only very good things could ever come.

Be here now. Be yourself fully. Embrace the power of the present moment, and welcome true joy and peace into your daily life. As Ralph Waldo Emerson wrote, we can never do a kindness too soon. Nor can we be grateful too soon, nor loving too soon, nor fully alive too soon. Indeed, now is the time. Now is always the time.

Love, Meredith x

Acknowledgements

This book has been made possible by the most exquisite collaboration of my life. I started to see stories in Roberto's sumptuous photographs from the first moment I laid my eyes on them. I saw and see so much in them.

Through such intelligent, sensitive and grateful eyes, Roberto captures the world around him. Most of these images were captured on adventures we have shared over the past two years — each adventure made all the more memorable by our shared documentation of the experience: an enriching, fulfilling and profound creative journey of life.

As the pictures for this book came together in a beautiful collection, my words flowed. As if speaking out loud, Roberto's photographs had something to say and I, a faithful and inspired scribe, did my utmost to translate these message into little observations for you — ways of looking at life with new eyes, ways to love life, commune with the magic of life and be here now — in peace, joy and gratitude. As they say, change the way you see things and the things you see change. We sincerely wish that this book will inspire you to see, and build upon that seeing as you craft an enchanting life you truly love.

It has been a privilege for me to bring this book to life with my humble and brilliant husband, and for it to be a vivid, life-affirming expression of not only our love but our shared passion for the beauty of life in its robust, delicate, intense and subtle splendour.

As we laid photographs into pages with words, like a journal, art came to life. Dipping inks, scribbly markers, pencils, crayons, little bits of letters, dried flowers and tiny, miscellaneous clippings all played a part. We are most grateful to the following people whose contribution to representing the lovingly hand-created pages of this book have made it what it is: Todd Rechner, Mick Smith, Ash Spicer, Jesse Wheeler, Tony Tong, Meaghan Thomson and Martin Barry. Heartfelt thanks to editors Allison Hiew and Antonietta Melideo for their thoughtfulness, time and care, and to designer Sarah Mawer for her attention to detail and truly beautiful approach.

We also express our sincere thanks to Sandy Grant, Pam Brewster and the entire team at Hardie Grant whose unanimous yes to this unique concept had us on our way. We appreciate your dedication to this project and the beauty of its production.

To our friends and families, to all those whose interest and care has touched this book, very much including you, dear reader, we offer our appreciation.

I am sincerely thankful for the inspiration I feel within and around me each day and, more than ever, I commit to being here now.

Love, Meredith x

Photo credit
Nick Burdon

Published in 2023 by Hardie Grant Books,
an imprint of Hardie Grant Publishing

Hardie Grant Books (Melbourne)
Building 1, 658 Church Street
Richmond, Victoria 3121

Hardie Grant Books (London)
5th & 6th Floors
52–54 Southwark Street
London SE1 1UN

hardiegrant.com/au/books

Hardie Grant acknowledges the Traditional Owners of the country on which we work, the Wurundjeri people of the Kulin nation and the Gadigal people of the Eora nation, and recognises their continuing connection to the land, waters and culture. We pay our respects to their Elders past and present.

Copyright text and illustrations © Meredith Gaston Masnata 2023
Copyright photography © Roberto Masnata 2023, except page 193 © Nick Burdon 2023
Copyright design © Hardie Grant Publishing 2023
Every effort has been made to trace, contact and acknowledge all copyright holders. Please contact the publisher with any information on errors or omissions.

Be Here Now
ISBN 978 1 74379 910 9

10 9 8 7 6 5 4 3 2 1

A catalogue record for this book is available from the National Library of Australia

Publisher: Pam Brewster
Editor: Allison Hiew
Design Manager: Kristin Thomas
Production Manager: Todd Rechner

Colour reproduction by Splitting Image Colour Studio
Printed in China by Leo Paper Products LTD.

The paper this book is printed on is from FSC®-certified forests and other sources. FSC® promotes environmentally responsible, socially beneficial and economically viable management of the world's forests.